Data-Driven Dialogue:

A Facilitator's Guide to Collaborative Inquiry

by
Bruce Wellman
Laura Lipton

 The Road To Learning

www.miravia.com

Page layout design by Michael Buckley with Lynne Schueler

Cover design by Michael Buckley

Data-Driven Dialogue:
A Facilitator's Guide to Collaborative Inquiry

by
Bruce Wellman and Laura Lipton

Permission for some materials in this book has been granted by the authors and/or publishers.

Permission for adaptation of materials from *New Horizons for Learning* website: *www.newhorizons.org* ©2003, New Horizons for Learning

We apologize for any oversights in obtaining permissions and would be happy to rectify them in future printings.

All Rights reserved. No part of this book may be copied, reproduced, translated or transmitted in any form or by any means, electronic or mechanical, including photocopying, recording, or by any information storage and retrieval system now known or to be developed, without written permission from the authors, except for the inclusion of brief quotations or for classroom educational purposes, or in connection with reviews.

Copyright © 2004 by MiraVia, LLC

10 9 8 7 6 5 4 3 2

Third printing, September, 2006

Printed in the United States of America

ISBN 0-9665022-3-x   Softcover

MiraVia, LLC • 3 Lost Acre Trail • Sherman CT 06784 *www.miravia.com*

And what is good, Phaedras,
And what is not good—
Need we ask anyone to tell us these things?
    Robert M. Pirsig; Zen and the Art of Motorcycle Maintenance

A TAPESTRY

Once, an idea
Intricately woven with care
   and love.

Hearts and hands and minds
   Combine
Artistry with craftsmanship;
   Invention with precision.

Fancy made real.
Reality made fancy.

Crafted on a loom of trust
   and acceptance,
Knowledge mixed with uncertainty,
   Reflection blended with humility,
     Passion tempered with humor.
Vibrant hues.
Shot through
With Questions,
   Gold, purple, deepest blue.

Patterns fold back upon themselves
   Creating new patterns
Imagination as infinite variety.

It shelters, but does not insulate.
Substantial, but never smothering
Replenishing with its warmth.

Almost so familiar as not to be noticed
It surprises and delights with its richness.

LEL

CONTENTS

APPENDIX

REFERENCES AND RESOURCES

INDEX

ABOUT THE AUTHORS

PROFESSIONAL DEVELOPMENT PROGRAMS AND SERVICES

PREFACE

"In large numbers of schools, and for long periods of time, teachers are colleagues in name only. They work out of sight and hearing of one another, plan and prepare their lessons and materials alone, and struggle on their own to solve most of their instructional, curricular and management problems. Against this almost uniform backdrop of isolated work, some schools stand out for the professional relationship they foster among teachers. These schools, more than others, are organized to permit the sort of reflection . . . that has been largely absent from professional preparation and professional work in schools. For teachers in such schools, work involves colleagueship of a more substantial sort. Recognition and satisfaction stem not only from being a masterful teacher, but also from being a member of a masterful group."

—Judith Warren Little

DATA HAVE NO MEANING

A fundamental premise of this book is the importance of engaging educational practitioners around tough-to-talk about topics in data-driven conversations. Essential to this collaborative inquiry is the use of data as the focus, and process skills as the means for exchanging viewpoints and building shared understandings. Meaning is imposed through interpretation. How we understand is subjective. Meaning is defined in and by relationship. Even words, up/down, large/ small, close/ far can only be defined contextually. A 5'11" individual is short if he or she is a member of a professional basketball team.

Consequently, in this world of abstractions, school leaders are wise to approach meaning making as an active, personal and social process. As such, the words we employ to describe subjective experiences create complex webs of meaning that beg to be explored. Data, in a variety of forms, calibrates our individual perspectives with a potential shared reality. Skilled facilitators shape collaborative cultures, creating structures and processes for understanding. In these forums, individual realities bounce and bump, nest and dovetail, coalescing ultimately in the cultural artifacts expressed as a shared meaning system. Without such intentionally organized opportunities, data becomes something to fear, and to defend against (see Table I.1).

This point was driven home to us in a conversation with the director of assessment for a medium-sized school system. She was perplexed and a bit stunned by the response she received during a meeting with a district committee charged with analyzing the performance of students in upper elementary mathematics. The data in her tables and graphs were accurate, comprehensive and clearly displayed, yet part way through her presentation, committee members interrupted to explain why the data didn't tell the whole story, which parts couldn't possibly be true and how the positive effects of their efforts were not reflected. What was intended as a well-reasoned, thoughtful and data-focused session rapidly dissolved into defensiveness, denial and distracting peripheral comments.

Our colleague's experience is not uncommon. In our work with school and district teams across North America, we find similar patterns and pitfalls. The quest for more data-based planning, problem solving, and decision making often stumbles against limited capacities for engaging in thoughtful interactions. Typically, groups lack process tools, collaborative communication skills, and habits of reflection for talking productively about hard-to-talk about topics. What seems rational on the surface runs headlong into emotional torrents and confusion. There is a press towards product over process, which often leads to limiting and limited plans. Data presented poorly or prematurely are then perceived as irrelevant or worse as oppressive.

CREATING CONFIDENT DATA USERS

Teachers blaze the path to knowledge generation when pairs, small groups and entire faculties intentionally and purposefully use data as a source for analyzing progress and proactively planning for improvement.

Collaborative school cultures infused with purposeful, data-driven inquiry operate with the assumption that teachers are generators of knowledge about their practice. Meetings become a forum for testing new ideas and exploring research findings in the context of that school. When educators systematically inquire into school or classroom-based issues and concerns, develop research designs, collect and analyze data from multiple sources and establish and implement plans for change, they plant the seeds of their own professional development. Teachers harvest these seeds in the successes of their students.

While many educators engage in rigorous reflection regarding their own work, most school cultures do not embrace organized, collaborative examination of practice. Thus, in many ways, data-driven dialogue is countercultural. There are a variety of reasons for the lack of collective engagement in problem posing and problem-solving. Foremost, perhaps, are the competing priorities for limited amounts of available time. Educators have responsibilities to their students and to their students' parents; they must perform a variety of administrative tasks and often complete mountains of required paperwork. Time and energy for professional, data-driven exchanges with colleagues must be carved from the hours assigned to these responsibilities. In addition, many classroom teachers feel inadequate about the technical and statistical knowledge and skills needed to effectively organize and analyze data. Others bemoan a lack of appropriate and accessible technology.

But perhaps the most imposing roadblock to a successful journey into data-driven inquiry are the ways in which data have been used. Typically, data are collected for delivery to 'someone else.' These unnamed others might include the district office, the local community, or next year's classroom teacher. They have not been used for self-assessment, problem solving, reflection nor discovery. Even worse, data are often used to intimidate and blame, rather than support and improve. Educators see data as something that needs to be gathered, organized and submitted to comply with district or state driven requirements, rather than as a tool for understanding and improving their own practice. Nancy Love (2001) and her colleagues describe this discrepancy as the difference

The real methodology for system change begins and ends with ongoing, authentic conversations about important questions.

—Tony Wagner

Table I-1: Guiding Assumptions for Data-Driven Collaborative Inquiry

Data have no meaning.	Data are simply information. Individuals and groups create meaning by organizing, analyzing and interpreting data. Interpretation is subjective; data are objective. Frames of reference, the way we see the world, influence the meaning we derive from the data we collect and select.
Knowledge is both a personal and a social construction.	Human beings are meaning-making organisms. Knowledge is socially constructed and individually integrated. We sift experience through personal and social filters, forming beliefs and ways of knowing. Individuals interact with information and with others to shape new understandings from our world and about our world.
There is a reciprocal influence between the culture of the workplace and the thinking and behavior of its members.	Like societies, organizations have cultures that determine modes of behavior. Cultural artifacts, symbols and rituals reflect and transmit acceptable and unacceptable patterns and practices for individuals and groups. The introduction of new behaviors opens opportunities for testing cultural boundaries and shifting organizational norms.
Understanding should precede planning.	When confronted with data, individuals and groups often assign causality and determine solutions without clear problem definitions. They seek the comfort of action rather than navigate the discomfort of ambiguity. Skilled groups cultivate purposeful uncertainty as a pathway to understanding before jumping into planning processes.
Cycles of inquiry, experimentation and reflection accelerate continuous growth and learning.	Learning occurs when we shift from professional certainty to conscious curiosity, from isolated individual to collaborative community member, and from passive technician to active researcher. The pursuit of meaningful questions arises from thoughtful data analysis, careful problem framing, and ongoing monitoring of gaps between goal achievement and current conditions.
Norms of data-driven collaborative inquiry generate continuous improvements in student learning.	That we talk in our schools is vitally important in these changing times. How we talk may be as important. Understanding emerges from thoughtful inquiry and dialogue about important matters. Such inquiry is driven by high-quality data derived from internal and external sources. Because data in and of themselves have no meaning, data alone leads to no action. Meaning and action result from collective processes that develop shared commitment to improved student learning.

The question is how do we come together and think and hear each other in order to touch, and be touched by, the intelligence we need?

—Jacob Needleman

between being 'data givers' and being 'data users.' The real work for school leadership is shaping the cultural conditions and facilitating the shift towards responsible, informed, collaborative data users.

ABOUT THIS BOOK

Given the current conditions and guiding assumptions outlined above and our experiences working closely with teachers and administrators struggling to make sense of their collective work, we present this volume as a toolkit for focusing and guiding collaborative inquiry, problem solving and planning efforts to improve student learning.

The book is designed and written to support both novice and more expert facilitators in their work with school teams. We offer guiding principles, practical tools, field-tested tips and a three-phase model for structuring and facilitating data-focused conversations. To find specific facilitator's tips offered throughout the text, look for this Facilitator's Tip icon.

When thoughtfully implemented, the tools and the model presented here will increase the sense of psychological safety for group members engaged in collaborative processes. The tools and the model will also provide guidance and increase the confidence and skills of facilitators charged with steering these processes.

What You'll Find

Beyond this Preface, this book is organized into eight sections, including six chapters and three sections of additional resources and information. Here is what you'll find.

Chapter One—Current Conditions: Why We Talk

This chapter presents a view of the current conditions and driving forces shaping school improvement efforts. Informed by the literature on leading change, this chapter illuminates some possibilities and pitfalls as practitioners struggle with continuous improvement.

Chapter Two—Facilitative Patterns: Crafting the Container

This chapter offers frameworks and tools for developing facilitative skill in orchestrating data-driven dialogue to support school improvement. Strategies and guidelines for creating and sustaining productive work groups and for using data to focus participant attention and energy are presented here. Tips for developing increased capacity for working groups, as well as learning guides for enhancing the skills of the facilitator are included.

Chapter Three—A Model for Collaborative Inquiry: How We Talk

A three-phase, question-driven model for structuring data-driven conversations, The Collaborative Learning Cycle, is presented in this chapter. The importance of structuring collaborative inquiry, the possibilities and liabilities of each phase, as well as their cognitive and affective intentions are offered here.

CHAPTER FOUR—A DATA PRIMER: HOW WE KNOW

"What are data?" "How do we choose what to collect?" "How do we connect our questions with the data that will inform them?" These are some of the questions addressed in this chapter on data basics. Examples of data sources for naming and framing problems, distinctions between qualitative and quantitative data, the need for multiple data sources and ideas for creating or selecting assessment instruments fill this chapter. Information on choosing and organizing visually vibrant data displays and for creating data focused conversations is found here as well.

CHAPTER FIVE—TOOLS FOR TEAMS

A wide array of tools for teams, each with facilitator instruction, process tips and group development strategies, are listed alphabetically in this chapter. The tools structure a variety of thinking processes and group member interactions with and around data. Each strategy description details essential management, monitoring and mediating functions for skillful facilitation. Applications, variations and extensions, as well as an index organizing the tools by intention, required time and ideal work group size make this chapter a practical resource for novice and experienced facilitators alike. Look for this blackline master icon indicating that a related reproducible resource is provided.

p xx

CHAPTER SIX—LEADING SYSTEMS: STRUCTURES AND CAPACITIES FOR CONTINUOUS SCHOOL IMPROVEMENT

Organized around a framework that elaborates critical components in complex systems, this chapter establishes the context for data-driven conversations as vital elements within collaborative cultures. This section describes and explores the organizational and individual capacities that support the technological and sociological infrastructures of productive, learning-focused systems.

REPRODUCIBLE RESOURCES

Maximize your use of preparation time. Find reproducible masters for creating overhead transparencies of task directions, reproducible worksheets, and other workshop and meeting support tools in this practical section.

APPENDIX

This Appendix provides technical information related to the topic of data-driven dialogue. Included are a glossary of technical terms related to assessment and statistical analysis, examples of survey questions, and planning designs for meetings of varying lengths.

Learning is a continuous journey. This section includes an array of print and web resources for further exploration of group development, facilitative mastery and data use in school improvement.

WHAT YOU WILL NOT FIND

This book is not a book about the technical skills necessary for data analysis related to school improvement processes. For example, it does not offer insight into data management systems or methods for statistically analyzing standardized tests. There are a number of excellent volumes in that area listed in the References and Resource section. Nor is this purely a book about facilitation, consensus building or shared decision-making. Again, the field is so wide and so deep we could not hope to do it justice here. However, you will find additional resources in the References and Resource section to extend and complement what you find here.

CHANGE IS INEVITABLE; GROWTH IS OPTIONAL

Change produces tension. We tend to become comfortable with the known and anxious with the unfamiliar. Nevertheless, the drive towards excellence requires that we take measure of where we are and contrast that assessment with where we want to be. Recognizing the gap offers a choice point; remain static or grow. For some groups, the gap is daunting. Achieving the vision seems impossible; changing the status quo seems hopeless. "If only" or "yes, but" reactions are rampant. "Sure we could teach every child to read at grade level if only there were more support from their parents" or "Yes, we could shift the schedule to increase opportunities for collaboration but we would have less time for academic prep." However, the gap between what is and what could be also offers a source of energy for growth. This creative tension is "the force that comes into play at the moment when we acknowledge a vision that is at odds with current reality" (Senge, 1990, p. 151). It is an energy we must capture, embrace and cultivate if we are to succeed in creating learning environments that meet the challenges of our times. The shift requires first that the school community is willing to take an honest assessment of the present. This book offers theoretical constructs and practical tips for analyzing the gaps, building cultures of collaboration, creating organizations that thrive in times of change, and inspiring educators to open-mindedly engage with each other to produce optimal learning for all of our students.

"When we do come together in schools, we do so filled with the fear of being judged because we are in the business of fixing, saving, advising, and setting each other straight. So we find ourselves in these false forms of community in which the things we need to do to generate knowledge together simply aren't done. They are too risky in school settings where there is so much fear that we don't tell each other the truth. Instead, we posture or play roles or withdraw into silence in order to stay safe. If we want to create viable alternatives to researchers lobbing information at us we have to come together in community to engage in difficult forms of discourse out of which shared knowledge is generated."

—Parker Palmer

CHAPTER ONE—*Current Conditions: Why We Talk*

"With increased accountability, American schools and the people who work in them are being asked to do something new—to engage in systematic, continuous improvement in the quality of the educational experience of students and to subject themselves to the discipline of measuring their success by the metric of students' academic performance. Most people who currently work in public schools weren't hired to do this work, nor have they been adequately prepared to do it either by their professional education or their prior experience in schools."   —Richard F. Elmore

CHANGE AND TRANSITIONS

The literature on school improvement and the processes of change is rich and ever expanding (Sarason, 1990; Evans, 1996; Fullan, 2001; and Schlechty, 2001). Change and the tensions of change are a constant presence in the life of school professionals. Some changes are planned systems improvements, such as curriculum revision processes. Some changes emerge as responses to observed needs such as special tutoring programs for struggling students. And some changes are thrust upon the schools by outside forces such as dramatic demographic shifts when new industries come to town and attract immigrant workers or refugee resettlement programs significantly alter student populations. Data analysis processes and patterns of collaborative inquiry are themselves significant changes. They are also practices that lead to additional changes.

DRIVING FORCES

A cluster of intertwining forces drives the need for focused collaborative practices in schools today. The four major shifts described in the text that follows will be ongoing influences on the work lives of the current generation of teachers and educational leaders. Each of these drivers challenges the operating assumptions of the current organizing principles in schools. Each of these drivers also challenges the ways that many teachers and administrators define themselves as professionals. For all of us who work in and around schools, our personal and collective navigation through these four shifts, or change drivers, may well determine our own professional sense of satisfaction and accomplishment (see Table 1.1).

Table 1.1: Four Driving Forces of School Change

SHIFTING FROM	SHIFTING TO
A teaching focus	A learning focus
Teaching as private practice	Teaching as collaborative practice
School improvement as an option	School improvement as a requirement
Accountability	Responsibility

THE SHIFT FROM A TEACHING FOCUS TO A LEARNING FOCUS IN SCHOOLS

In a teaching-focused model, the act of teaching takes center stage. The teacher is the organizer and presenter of content, directing student attention toward discrete elements to be mastered and tested at prescribed intervals. In teaching-focused models, assessments are measures of learning, not tools for learning (Black and Wiliam, 1998). The basic operating assumption is that individual educators equipped with sufficient knowledge and skills will cumulatively serve the needs of successive groups of students. The teaching-focused model also assumes that a well-designed curriculum will coordinate and align the efforts of these isolated, semi-autonomous individuals within and across grade levels and content areas.

In emerging learning-focused models, the needs of learners and an emphasis on learning processes drive improvement efforts (Wiggins and McTighe, 1998; Bransford, Brown, & Cocking, 1999; and Lipton and Wellman, 2000). These approaches require sensitivity to student needs, timely information about individual and collective performances, and an appreciation for the often messy and nonlinear nature of learning and understanding. Teaching for understanding is profoundly different from teaching for coverage. Guidance comes from the learners and from the teacher's own cohesive understanding of the structure of the academic discipline being explored, not from a manual or lesson plan book (Shulman, 1987). This shift in practice requires attention to patterns of instruction and the social learning climate created in each classroom and across classrooms, teams and grade levels. In such student-centered approaches, the need for both curriculum and instructional alignment is paramount. How teachers teach is as much the curriculum as what teachers teach. This synergy of shared instructional repertoire across classrooms is only possible when teachers gather together to make meaning of their collective efforts and collective results.

In learning-focused models, assessments are tools for learning. Ongoing and embedded formative assessments guide in-flight lesson and unit designs informing daily instructional decisions. These assessment data become important points for analysis within and between classrooms. The search for patterns of success and the gap analysis between desired outcomes and current student performance organizes improvement efforts within class and between classrooms.

THE SHIFT FROM TEACHING AS PRIVATE PRACTICE TO TEACHING AS COLLABORATIVE PRACTICE

Individual teachers, no matter how gifted or dedicated, cannot work in isolation and produce the quality results possible from team planning and action. As schools and districts hone the crafts of assessment and data literacy, images of collective effect emerge in the charts and graphs. These patterns are the consequences of how schools are organized, what is talked about, who makes curricular and instructional decisions and how these decisions are made.

Historically, most reform efforts have concentrated on the behaviors and repertoires of individual teachers. This approach assumes that isolated and interchangeable teachers are the locus of change. The thinking that guides these efforts is deeply embedded in our culture. It is rooted in a collective notion of the 'real' classroom, with an autonomous teacher who has his or her way of doing things and who often has favorite units personally developed and honed over years of teaching (Tyack and Cuban, 1995; Lortie, 1975).

Teaching as collaborative practice operates with both a different set of assumptions and with different patterns of practice. When teachers operate in professional communities and take collective responsibility for student learning they produce school-wide gains in academic achievement (Louis, Kruse & Marks, 1996). Reflective dialogue about important matters is at the heart of such communities. In these schools, teaching and learning are public acts to be shared, examined, analyzed, and refined.

The tension between privacy norms and the drive towards more collaborative practice will increasingly be influenced by performance pressures from within the organization and cultural pressures from outside. From within, as performance data links to cross discipline and cross grade instructional patterns, difficult but necessary conversations will push their way onto the agenda.

At the same time, work life outside of schools is steadily shifting to collaborative and team-based models. These emerging cultural patterns in other professions will begin to influence school designs and models of how education professionals interact with one another. For example, McLaughlin and Talbert (2001) propose that high school teachers are likely to be influenced by the work environments of the disciplines that they teach. To truly teach a discipline, one has to explore the ways in which knowledge is produced in that field.

Elements of Teachers' Professional Community

1. *Shared norms and values*
2. *Collective focus on student learning*
3. *Collaboration*
4. *Deprivatized practice*
5. *Reflective dialogue*

—Louis, Kruse, & Marks, 1996

THE SHIFT FROM SCHOOL IMPROVEMENT AS AN OPTION TO SCHOOL IMPROVEMENT AS A REQUIREMENT

In a climate of increased accountability and official expectations, responsibility for teaching and learning goals has shifted from the classroom to legislative offices and education departments. The demand for clear and measurable performance standards with associated high stakes assessment systems significantly impacts the operating norms of districts, schools, and classrooms. Within this climate, many states and provinces now require planning teams as part of their ongoing school improvement efforts.

While these efforts are usually well intentioned, these policies often establish a climate of fear and a sense of loss of control over daily work for educators. To regain a sense of personal and collective power over learning outcomes requires both collaborative skills and emotional readiness to engage productively with data. These skills and attitudes support exploration and understanding of the patterns that produce the measured results. They are also fundamental to planning and implementing appropriate changes in practice. The need for academic and instructional goal clarity amplifies the need for cohesive, shared efforts. This focus emerges from a school's ability to organize, analyze, problem solve and plan with data (Fuhrman, 1999).

Improvement is a *discipline* in the true sense of that word, requiring training and the perfection of skills that produce desired characteristics, behaviors and outcomes. Improvement is not an activity or a committee assignment. It is an essential form of professional and organizational engagement that calls forth expertise and dispositions for learning and productive adult interaction.

THE SHIFT FROM ACCOUNTABILITY TO RESPONSIBILITY

Schools are not the only institutions in our society feeling the pressures of measurement and performance goals. Richard Elmore points out that, "In other high skill, knowledge-based occupations—research and development, engineering, health care, even social services—some system of evaluation and accountability has been an important part of professional life for at least two decades. So when educators claim that they are being unfairly treated by a hostile accountability system, it's not surprising that people who work in other knowledge-intensive sectors are not particularly sympathetic" (Elmore, 2002, p. 4).

Some form of accountability is the new reality for educational professionals. The choice is not whether to be accountable but rather what forms that accountability will take and how individuals and organizations will respond to these new conditions.

Increased organizational transparency will be a dominant feature of this new environment. Transparency is fast becoming a fact of life for both public and private sector organizations. Open meetings, open books and a free press are all forms of organizational and political transparency. Information processing technology will accelerate this trend in schools. Databases linking student assessments, demographic information and teacher grade books will open the system to a widening range of observers and potential participants in problem solving efforts.

Systems become self-correcting when everyone can see the moving parts, leading to earlier problem detection and earlier intervention. To make systems self-correcting means that individual educators need to learn to see the systems of which they are a part. They will also need to learn how to analyze, plan and implement improvement efforts at the systems level and to think beyond the boundaries of their classroom or schoolhouse doors.

Accountability is often perceived as a coerced response to outside agents. In low performing schools, accountability is something that is done to the school, not an energy that drives the school from within. In such schools, especially those that lack collaborative norms and capacities, external data bounce off cultures of isolationism. All school staffs need the skills and ability to turn raw data from many different sources into meaningful information that they and others understand and can act with and act upon (Newman, King, & Rigdon, 1997).

An organizing value for the goal of developing habits of collaborative inquiry within schools is to build a sense of internal accountability or, we suggest, a sense of internal responsibility within individuals and within the organization. The shift from accountability to responsibility means that teachers and school leaders make the shift from depending on others to do the analysis, to becoming proactive data users and analysts themselves (Love, 2002). Responsibility carries with it a sense of duty and obligation to students and colleagues, with the embedded notion of a promise to work toward results and a commitment to ongoing professional and organizational improvement efforts.

One important form of professional responsibility is the responsibility to spread effective practices throughout a school. As the work of William Sanders and his colleagues (Sanders and Rivers, 1996) has demonstrated, when student performance is measured by assessments that have a strong relationship to the curriculum, there is often greater teacher-to-teacher variation within a school than there is school-to-school variation within a district or region. In one study of mathematics achievement, highly effective teachers produced learning gains as much as 50 percentile points greater than the gains reported for matched sets of students taught by less effective teachers.

This work emphasizes the impact of successive teachers on student learning. In their study on teacher effects, Sanders and colleagues found that vastly different academic outcomes can result for students of

Accountability: answerable, From the Latin, cunter, compter—to count, to compute, and from Old French, acunter, accomputare— to count up, to reckon.

Responsibility: a duty, an obligation, to promise in return, capable of making moral or rational decisions on one's own and therefore answerable for one's behavior. From the Latin. Respondere, to respond, obligation.

comparable ability, depending upon the sequence of teachers to which they are assigned. Students who have a sequence of ineffective teachers in their early grades will suffer a residual effect in performance, no matter how effective their subsequent teachers.

Developing patterns and practices of responsibility for the learning of all students in the school carries with it layers of meaning. In the end, a slight shift in spelling may carry the most important message of all to individual teachers, teams, departments and staffs. That spelling shift is from *responsibility* to *response-ability*. When we accept the notion that the way we currently respond to student learning needs produces current results, we come to realize that if we want different results we will have to learn to respond differently. These responses will need to occur at both the instructional and organizational level if we want more students to reach greater and deeper levels of learning.

Each of these four drivers requires psychological reorientation for individual educators and for the ways in which they interact professionally. Given the interconnected nature and simultaneity of these drivers, collective processes for meaning making, problem solving and planning are essential resources within schools and districts.

PSYCHOLOGICALLY REORIENTING TO CHANGE

While change is a constant in our society and in our institutions, the response to change is always local and highly personal. The work of William Bridges (1990) is a useful guide in this arena. He emphasizes that change is a given and ultimately is not the problem. His work focuses on transitions, which he defines as the psychological reorientation to the changes that are occurring. This reorientation requires shifts in the ways in which we define our work, our organizations and ourselves. Transitions have three phases: an ending, a neutral zone and a new beginning. Given the many changes that are occurring in schools, different change processes and different people in the organization may be at any of these stages at a given point in time. To successfully navigate transitions, individuals and organizations need maps and tools. Bridges' three phases provide one such map.

Endings

Endings as cultural milestones are often overlooked. They must be framed concretely and symbolically. Many improvement efforts stall when people in the organization have not yet let go of former ways of doing business. Changes in curriculum and instruction are often resisted when what is ending is not clearly named and marked. For planners, a key question is, "Who is losing what in this change?" Often the loss is one of confidence and professional certainty. As states, provinces and districts adopt clear learning standards connected to performance-based assessment systems, many veteran teachers feel the loss of autonomy and the choice of what to teach and when to teach it. Favorite units, refined over many years of teaching get squeezed out of the official curriculum. To many educators, it feels as if the rules have been altered in the middle of the game.

Neutral Zone

The neutral zone is often a time of anxiety and uneasiness. New patterns have not yet emerged, old patterns are slipping away or have been abolished and the day-to-day comforts of established routines may be too fragile a resource for maintaining personal and professional equilibrium. Curriculum change is a prime example of this phase in action. The new conceptually oriented mathematics programs bring this phase to the foreground (Schoenfeld, 2002). Teachers' own mathematical knowledge is often stretched by these curriculums. Teaching and learning success requires a grasp of the whole program with its embedded instructional strategies. Teachers cannot learn these programs one lesson at a time or be successful trying to stay one lesson ahead of their students. Work cultures that support and honor the learning processes of individual professionals help to ease the tensions of the neutral zone.

New Beginnings

At the point of new beginnings, William Bridges reminds us that leaders need to sell the problem and not the solution. One of the most important uses of data is for problem finding and to develop problem understanding and ownership. Collective ownership of problems and issues results from shared exploration of data, both the quantitative measures from formal assessments and the qualitative measures of student work samples and student performances. Without such well-structured processes leaders may find themselves attempting to sell solutions to people who don't own problems.

The Collaborative Learning Cycle described in Chapter Three presents a scaffold for group investigation, discovery and action planning. It is through collective processes of inquiry and analysis that groups move toward consensus about what needs to end in the curricular and instructional approaches that are producing the data under consideration, embrace the tensions and possibilities of the neutral zone and find their own new beginnings. The following chapter offers an extensive toolkit for facilitating the critical conversations and developing the cultural norms that produce learning-focused organizations ready to navigate the seas of change.

Notes

CHAPTER TWO—Facilitative Patterns: Crafting the Container

"The importance of small groups has never been more clear: From the day we are born with the help of a "birthing group" to the day we are mourned by a group of family and friends, small groups are woven into the fabric of our individual lives, while at the collective level, from the classroom to the courtroom, they are the stitches that hold together the communal cloth. . . . In a fragmented world, the small group [is] the generative site at which individuals and collectives such as organizations and institutions are made and remade."

—Lawrence R. Frey

Humans are a social species with roots in a primate past. The physical and social environment shaped our early ancestors mentally and emotionally. Like our predecessors, we are attuned to the cues of others and are predisposed to take collective action when it serves the greater good.

Yet, there is really no such thing as a group. Groups emerge from collections of individuals who make choices about how and when to participate. All groups and group members have boundaries formed by physical, technical, temporal and social elements (Arrow and McGrath, 1993). These boundaries are the membranes through which information and resources flow in and out of a group. The words membrane and member share related Latin roots—'membrana', meaning the skin covering an organ or member of the body and 'membrum', a limb or body that is a distinct part of the whole. At one level, group members are the bodies enclosed within the boundaries of a membrane. At another level, each member has his or her own boundaries—his or her own membranes.

In the study of physical science, we learn that membranes can be permeable, semi-permeable, or impermeable to various size molecules. Gortex ™ fabric is an example of these attributes in action. This material is permeable to the molecules of human body perspiration—it breathes. At the same time, the fabric is impermeable to the larger water molecules of rain and snow—it is waterproof. In the same ways, the boundaries of groups and of group members vary in permeability. The key difference is that these boundaries are not fixed physical properties. Skilled facilitation and purposeful group development open these membranes within and between people, information and insight.

The work of groups is the work of boundary shifting, knowing when to focus in and when to focus out. It is the work of seeking information, processing information, decision making, planning and implementation. These tasks are also the work of individuals operating within the membrane of the group. The work of group development is the work of helping members see their parts within the whole and helping group members take responsibility for regulating their personal and collective permeability to ideas, options and actions.

*W*hat has been discovered is that, first, people will not voluntarily share knowledge unless they feel some moral commitment to do so; second, people will not share knowledge unless the dynamics of change favor exchange; and third, data without relationships merely cause more information glut. Put another way, turning information into knowledge is a social process, and for that you need good relationships. —Michael Fullan

GROUP DEVELOPMENT

Group

Development

- *Attention to task*

- *Attention to process*

- *Attention to relationship*

Productive groups learn from experience by setting goals for themselves, monitoring their performance and reflecting on their practice. Experience by itself is not a reliable teacher. By focusing only on the tasks at hand, groups may complete that task but do not expand their capacities for doing harder or more sophisticated work.

The harnesses of draft horses are fitted with blinders to block peripheral vision and keep the horse's attention on the road or furrow ahead. Many groups operate with similar blinders when they do not attend to organizing their tasks to increase their efficiency and productivity; when they do not attend to developing their process toolkit for supporting thinking and clear communication; and when they do not attend to developing relationships within the group to build their capacities for collaboration and strengthening professional community (see Appendix B: Group Development Rubric).

ATTENTION TO TASK

Productive groups plan for and monitor the following task dimensions, making necessary adjustments to improve their practices:

- Task designs are learning-focused: the group establishes task priorities that are congruent with organizational values, uses data to focus its attention and energy, and relates specific tasks to larger systems issues and frameworks.

- Task designs are time and energy efficient: the group establishes and maintains clear task and product success criteria, establishes and maintains clear task agendas, and uses data effectively to make decisions.

- Task designs are data-driven: the group collects and selects relevant data for its work, develops and utilizes effective data displays, and uses data effectively to make decisions.

ATTENTION TO PROCESS

Productive groups plan for and monitor the following process dimensions, making necessary adjustments to improve practices:

- Process aware groups develop shared tools and structures: the group applies tools and structures for focusing its tasks, follows agreed upon protocols, and refocuses if members deviate from task agreements or process guidelines.

- Process aware groups structure learning-focused conversations: group members invite and sustain the thinking of others by pausing, paraphrasing and inquiring, give their full attention to others through eye contact, listen nonjudgmentally and listen without interrupting; balance advocacy for their own ideas with inquiry into the ideas of others.

- Process aware groups structure data-driven dialogue: the group uses data to focus and calibrate conversations, inquires into and clarifies its own and others' assumptions, and seeks shared understanding of ideas, opinions and perspectives.

ATTENTION TO RELATIONSHIP

Productive groups balance task and process dimensions with equal attention to developing the group as a whole.

- Relationships grow when: shared norms and values ensure psychological safety for all group members, group members behave congruently with agreed upon norms and filter choices and decisions through agreed upon values.

- Relationships grow when: participation is balanced and contributions from others are encouraged, group members seek and honor diverse perspectives and anticipate and accept that productive conflict contributes to group success.

- Relationships grow and professional community develops when: individual and collective teaching practices are actively questioned and calibrated against clear and agreed upon standards, and group members engage purposely with relevant tasks that are focused on student learning and consistently use data to self assess and reflect.

CRAFTING THE CONTAINER

Skilled groups and skilled facilitators craft a conversational container within which it is psychologically safe to discover, to learn and to not have to be certain. Within this container are three important elements.

STRATEGIES FOR STARTING THE CONVERSATION

Groups don't automatically come to the table and begin work. Most group members are making a physical, emotional and cognitive transition from other activities to the session they are joining. Effective strategies for starting the conversation center group members' attention on a common point of focus. Such strategies also enhance affective and cognitive resources as foundations for group work and group member learning. In addition to the Four Box and Visual Synectics strategies found in Chapter Five, see Appendix D: Strategies for Getting Started.

PROTOCOLS FOR STRUCTURING THE CONVERSATION

Purposeful conversations require shape and structure. Groups tend to avoid hard-to-talk-about topics when they lack protocols and processes for structuring data-driven dialogue and data-driven discussion. External structures maximize efficient use of time and increase psychological safety for individual group members. The Collaborative Learning Cycle described in the next chapter offers a practical approach to structuring data-based inquiry.

VERBAL AND NONVERBAL TOOLS FOR SUSTAINING THINKING IN THE CONVERSATION

Participants make moment-to-moment decisions about whether or not a given instance is psychologically safe enough to risk offering a response, insight, or question. The facilitator's nonverbal and verbal communication skills are an important and modifiable factor in these participant decisions. The nonverbal and verbal skills of participants also influence one another. Later in this chapter we explore this tool set from both the perspective of group members and the perspective of facilitators.

SAFETY VERSUS COMFORT

Safety and comfort are not always the same thing in collaborative settings. Comfort with other people's discomfort is an important facilitator resource. It is not the facilitator's responsibility to make everyone feel at ease at all times. If groups are talking about the right things, individuals and the entire group may be unsettled at points in the conversation. The facilitator's responsibility is to protect the integrity of the process being used and provide safety and security for group members by helping them to trust that process.

Crafting the
Container
- *Starting the*
  conversation
- *Structuring the*
  conversation
- *Sustaining*
  thinking in the
  conversation

Skilled facilitators
offer the
- *'What'*
- *'Why'*
- *'How'*
of strategies and
protocols

PRESENT THE WHAT, WHY AND HOW

Skilled facilitators keep a group emotionally resourceful by presenting the 'what', 'why', and 'how' of strategies and protocols. When giving directions to a group, explain *what* you are going to do, your intentions or purpose for the task—*why* you're asking them to do this, and then the *how* or specific directions. These three factors offer group members structure, rationale and procedures for task engagement, increasing their willingness to engage productively.

A MENTAL MODEL FOR FACILITATION

Skilled facilitators employ a three layer mental model to guide their actions. They 'anticipate', they 'monitor' and they 'recover' when necessary. Given the improvisatory nature of conducting meetings and collaborative inquiry sessions, a repertoire of emotional and physical moves for recovery is a facilitator's stock in trade (see Table 2.1).

This three-layer macro lens, informs design and preparation before sessions, observation, analysis, decisions and actions during sessions and reflection and goal setting after sessions.

Conversational containers may be fragile or robust depending on the awareness and skills of group members. When group members have had little experience with a process or their confidence in each other is low, facilitators need to take special care in crafting the container. Task and process clarity are vital when emotions may be clouding the attention and perceptions of group members. The facilitator's nonverbal messages are as important as the verbal messages in developing task and process clarity and in establishing and maintaining a psychologically safe environment (Grinder, 1997).

Skilled facilitators

- *Anticipate*
- *Monitor*
- *Recover*

Table 2.1: A Mental Model for Facilitation

Skilled facilitators employ a three layer mental model to guide their actions.	
They anticipate	• the emotional state of groups with which they will be working
	• the room arrangements and physical materials required for task success
	• their own emotional readiness and the internal resources they will need to stay focused and centered
They monitor	• group member nonverbal and verbal responses
	• group member compliance with task and process protocols
	• their own emotional resourcefulness
They recover	• when group members lose emotional resourcefulness
	• when miscommunication and task or process confusion emerges
	• when they lose their own emotional resourcefulness

There is more than a verbal tie between the words common, community, and communication. [People] live in a community by virtue of the things they have in common; and communication is the way in which they come to possess things in common.

—John Dewey

GETTING PERMISSION TO FACILITATE

Facilitators and group members negotiate a tacit contract during each session in which they interact. During this negotiation group members determine whether or not they will give a facilitator full permission to organize and orchestrate their activities. Permission to facilitate is not derived by role. The emotional state of the group, the time of day and the topics at hand are just some of the variables that might influence a group's decisions. Group member engagement, cooperation and willingness to take emotional and cognitive risks are the major manifestations of their agreement to follow the facilitator's lead.

Facilitators need two types of permission from groups

- *Permission to direct process*
- *Permission to place issues before the group*

Facilitators need two types of permission. The first is permission to direct the group processes that will manage the meeting's content and topics. The second type is permission to place issues before the group (Grinder, 1997). These issues might be guiding questions, problem statements, action plans, or data for analysis.

Several factors influence group member responses. These include the facilitator's relationship to the group in terms of role or power, and group member perceptions of the facilitator's investment in specific outcomes for the session. If the facilitator is the formal supervisor of any of the group members, prior experiences with being open and honest about uncertainties will strongly influence how individuals participate in collaborative inquiry and in data-driven dialogue. If it was safe to be uncertain in earlier situations with that supervisor then it may be safe again in this new setting. If the facilitator has specific content area responsibilities and has been promoting a specific program of action, it may be difficult for a group to engage in collaborative analysis and problem finding, particularly if the data hint at low performance or lack of successful implementation.

Two key facilitation strategies that increase a group's willingness to give permission to their facilitator are role clarification and role negotiation.

ROLE CLARIFICATION

Experienced facilitators open sessions by clarifying their role and responsibilities. They name their intentions to frame and orchestrate the processes that will guide the group and they name their intention to stay neutral about the content and not evaluate contributions (Doyle and Straus, 1976).

ROLE NEGOTIATION

One approach to empowering a working group, whether it is at a novice level of performance as a group or at a more expert level, is to negotiate your stance as a facilitator. Stances may vary from hard to soft facilitation. An effective way to offer these options is to describe a physical continuum organized by metaphors, then ask group members to point to the spot on the continuum they believe will be most effective for that session. Some metaphors that we have used include facilitation stances that range from Rambo to Mr. Rogers; from Xena Warrior Princess to Mary Poppins; or from a lion to a lamb. Presenting choices helps the group to gain or regain the power to control its own direction and purposes. This is especially true if individual group members are dominating the group's time and energies. Such a group will tend to select harder forms of facilitation and give the facilitator permission to intervene with problematic situations.

 CHOOSE VOICE

Master teacher and teacher educator, Michael Grinder, stresses the importance and effectiveness of operating along a vocal range that runs from a credible to an approachable tone. Facilitators who have intonational versatility can choose an inflectional pattern that is congruent with their intention, thus sending clear messages and maintaining trust. A credible voice communicates confidence and believability, while an approachable voice is the voice of relationship and the voice that signals psychological safety. Practice with this vocal repertoire by tucking your chin slightly to achieve the tight modulation of the credible voice. Push your chin up to achieve the rising inflectional ending of the approachable voice (see Table 2.2).

Table 2.2: Choose Voice

VOICE	WHAT IT DOES	WHAT ITS USED FOR	PHYSICAL ELEMENTS
Credible	Communicates confidence and believability	• focusing individual group member's attention toward the group, specific items, and locations in the room • direction giving, such as framing topics and protocols for interaction • emphasizing important content information	• a narrow range of vocal modulation • a dropping of the chin and shoulders to relax the neck and muscles of the diaphragm • holding the head still • leaning back slightly • and for some individuals, a slight tilt of the chin for relationship
Approachable	The voice of relationship and the voice that signals psychological safety	• stimulating participant responses • paraphrasing group member responses • asking mediational questions to open and focus thinking	• a wider range of modulation than the credible voice • eye contact with participants • movement of the head • leaning towards the group to close the space

THREE POINT COMMUNICATION

Again from Michael Grinder, we learn the importance of establishing a third point for conversations. Third points might include professional articles or text selections, samples of student work or displays of quantitative or qualitative data. This non-verbal strategy establishes a triangle, with the facilitator as one point, the group as a second point, and the data, or focusing information as the third point (see Figure 2.1). The focus on the third point increases psychological safety, separating the information from the facilitator and allowing group members to talk with and about the data without having to make eye contact with colleagues. Skilled facilitators aid this process by depersonalizing the information under consideration. They do so by using impersonal language to describe the information—the data, this information, that chart, the article, the student work—instead of using personal pronouns to describe information—your students' work, our results, your test scores. The goal is to turn data and information into a 'thing'. It is much easier to talk about 'things' than it is to talk about 'us'. Several of the paired and small group tools in Chapter Five rely on this third point notion for exploring text. In these cases the shared text becomes the third point between partners that supports deeper conversations among colleagues. The Collaborative Learning Cycle described in the next chapter centers on large shared data displays that provide visually vibrant third points.

Figure 2.1: Third Point

DEFINING GROUP FACILITATION

Facilitation is planned improvisation. Like skilled dancers, musicians or actors, facilitators draw upon deeply embedded knowledge and a repertoire of moves grounded in experience and the wisdom of craft.

Good facilitation often goes unnoticed. The term facilitator means to make easier and to free from difficulties or obstacles. When this occurs adroitly, the group's attention is on its work and not on the facilitator or on what the facilitator is doing. In this way, the facilitator helps a group to recognize that the group itself is responsible for its actions and outcomes and that it is not the facilitator's group or the facilitator's success.

Expert facilitators help groups manage the tensions of task completion, process skills enhancement and group development. Doyle and Straus (1976) refer to the task and process tensions as balancing the "gum and chew" ratio. Gum comes in two forms: one form is cognitive; the other form is emotional. Different tasks place varying levels of cognitive and emotional demands upon group members. With these factors in mind, the skillful facilitator offers strategies and structures to help group members chew their way through the gum of a given session. Along the way, good facilitators make process commercials to extend group member skills and structure reflective moments to promote personal and collective awareness that in turn supports the development of the group as a whole.

INVITING THINKING

The human brain is wired to detect threat in the communications of others. Incoming sensory data from the eyes and ears are filtered by the emotional processing centers of the limbic brain. These signals travel first in the brain to the thalamus, which acts as a switching center and then across a single synapse to the amygdala where messages are checked against emotional memories and analyzed for degree of danger. If no threat is detected, signals then travel through a second circuit to the neocortex where higher-level cognitive operations occur (Goleman, 1994). Biological reactions take place in split seconds. These brain/body responses have served our species well across the millennia. In more modern times they may also inhibit thoughtfulness and creativity in collaborative settings if facilitators and participants are not conscious of the ways in which their communication patterns influence others. Group members must feel a sense of emotional safety before they can produces cognitive complexity. Both facilitators and group members need awareness of the need for and the skills for inviting thinking from others. Shared cognition is the essence of group work.

By attending to the following invitational elements facilitators and group members can *anticipate, monitor* and *recover* if group members appear to be confused, insecure or unwilling to respond to directions and questions.

ATTENDING FULLY

The invitation begins with physical attention to others to signal that our full presence is available for this conversation and that we intend no harm. This physical message meshes with several important verbal elements that compose an invitation to think together and to think about the various ideas and or data being explored.

Inviting Thinking

- *Attending Fully*
- *Approachable Voice*
- *Plural Forms*
- *Exploratory Language*
- *Nondichotomous Questions*
- *Positive Presuppositions*

APPROACHABLE VOICE

The use of an approachable voice, described above, is the first verbal element in the invitation. This tonal package wraps around a facilitator's or group member's comments, to indicate the intention to invite and explore thinking. An approachable voice is well modulated and tends to rise at the end of the statement, paraphrase or question.

PLURAL FORMS

Two important syntactical choices invite colleagues to think with us and increase the options and possibilities for thinking. The first is to use plural forms; *observations* instead of *observation, option*s instead of *option.* The use of plural forms sets aside the need for evaluation and the sorting of ideas. Often, group members need to hear their ideas aloud before they know which are most central to the issues before the group.

EXPLORATORY LANGUAGE

The second syntactical element is the use of exploratory phrasing in statements, paraphrases and questions. Words like *some, might, seems, possible,* and *hunches* widen the potential range of response and reduce the need for confidence and surety. Words like *could* and *why* may decrease the confidence of listeners by seeming to ask for premature commitment or a need to defend ideas and actions that are not yet fully developed.

Some examples of exploratory language include:

"So, you're noticing several different factors *might* be influencing the student performance data you are examining."

"What are *some* of the things that you are observing in this sample of student work?"

"You *seem* to have *some hunches* about what might need to happen next."

"Given these proposals, *what are some* criteria you *might* develop for making your selection?"

POSITIVE PRESUPPOSITIONS

All language carries embedded presuppositions (Elgin, 2000). These presuppositions are not always apparent in the words used but are present in the underlying assumptions communicated to the listener of that language. Positive presuppositions communicate a belief in group members' capacities and on-going willingness to engage with each other and with ideas.

For example, a group member might say, "Our students just can't do this work." A facilitator or another group member might respond with

*S*yntactical
Substitutions

- *the—some*

- *could—might*

- *is—seems*

- *why—what*

the paraphrase, "So, you're concerned about helping all of these students be successful." As a facilitator, instead of asking a group, "Can anyone see any patterns in this data?" you might ask "As you examine this data set, what are some of the things that you are noticing?"

NONDICHOTOMOUS QUESTIONS

Invitational and mediational facilitators and group members frame their questions using the elements listed above. In addition, they frame their questions by using open-ended, nondichotomous forms. These are questions that cannot be answered yes or no. For example, instead of asking a group, "Did anyone notice anything unusual in this data set?" they ask, "What are some interesting or unusual things that you noticed in this data set?" By eliminating dichotomous stems such as, "Can you," "Did you," "Will you," or "Have you," facilitators and skilled group members invite productive thinking and communicate a further level of positive expectations.

INTERNALIZE INVITATIONAL PATTERNS

Inquiry is one of the facilitator's most important resources. To facilitate means to make easier. Well-crafted questions that open individual and group member thinking make thinking easier by framing what to think about and some approaches for thinking by offering cognitive cues. Automatize the invitational patterns of your language to make conversations and work sessions psychologically safe and cognitively rich. When you anticipate anxiety for yourself or on the part of a group, it is often helpful to script some questions before the session to ensure these invitational qualities. Use the mediational questions embedded in the Collaborative Learning Cycle (see Chapter Three) as samples to guide your thinking.

BLOCKS TO UNDERSTANDING

Individuals reared in Western culture develop the often counter-productive notion that the prime way that one contributes to a conversation is by speaking or interjecting. This form of participation leads to meetings in which group members are either talking or waiting to talk. Silence doesn't necessarily equate to listening. Often, silent individuals may have either mentally checked out or are composing their next utterance.

As groups develop they come to realize that listening to others may be the single most important behavior in which group members engage. To listen deeply, with full attention, requires energy and a commitment to the processes of the group. Listening carefully to others also involves monitoring our own internal processes and developing awareness and control over several common internal distractions. These internal distractions or blocks to understanding shift our listening focus inward, to our own opinions, interests and surety about potential solutions. This shift to self distracts us from understanding others.

'I' LISTENING

Listening through the lenses of our own worldview diminishes our capacity to understand the perceptions and concerns of others. There are three specific categories of 'I' listening: personal referencing, personal curiosity, and personal certainty.

'I' Listening

Be Aware Of:

- *Personal Referencing*
- *Personal Curiosity*
- *Personal Certainty*

PERSONAL REFERENCING. Personal referencing is 'me too' or 'I would never' listening. It occurs when our minds shift from listening to understanding others to considering what is being said with reference to our own experiences. 'Me too' listening motivates serial story telling around the table consuming much of the time in typical meetings. The other form of personal referencing, 'I would never' listening, triggers internal assessment filters that can then lead to judgmental responses.

PERSONAL CURIOSITY. Personal curiosity drives our listening when we are interested in what others are saying, not to understand their perceptions and perspectives but because we want more information for ourselves. Our own curiosity and desire for details, whether or not it is relevant to the greater discussion, promotes egocentric questions and a personal search for information. This behavior may be at the expense of the group's agenda and process agreements.

PERSONAL CERTAINTY. Personal certainty blocks our listening when we feel sure that our perspective, insight or solution is the answer that the group is waiting for. This type of listening occurs when we prematurely stop attending outwardly and turn our attention to our own internal catalog of resources, viewpoints and solutions. Personal certainty leads to advice giving either directly or disguised in the form of questions such as, "Have you thought about . . . ?" "Has anyone noticed that . . . ?"

Facilitators need to be aware of their own patterns of listening. The blocks to understanding may be present for them as well. How a facilitator listens matters to how he or she is able to focus and how he or she is able to help a group and group members focus.

 INTERVENING WITH 'I' LISTENING

If you notice that some forms of 'I' listening have taken hold in a group, intervene by gently asking the following questions:

- "How much detail do you need to move forward with this item?" (This interrupts excessive storytelling and elaboration.)

- "How many of you are interested enough in this topic to stick with it at this point in time?" (This interrupts lines of questioning driven by personal curiosity.)

- "How many of you are still exploring possibilities here and are not yet ready to move to solutions or proposals for action?" (This interrupts personal certainty and advice giving.)

Group members who give their full attention to others contribute to relationship, clear communication and more productive work sessions. Patterns of collaborative inquiry and the habits of data-driven dialogue are built upon a foundation of listening. How we listen to others and how they listen to us, establishes a relationship between and among group members and between and among ideas.

LEARNING-FOCUSED VERBAL TOOLS

The verbal tools described in the following section are vital resources for facilitators and group members. Honing this toolkit is an essential task for individuals and groups that wish to improve their productivity and their relationships.

Within the invitational package described above, skilled facilitators and skilled group members *anticipate, monitor* and *recover* by applying the following verbal tools:

PAUSING to provide a space for thinking.

PARAPHRASING to establish relationships and increase understanding.

QUESTIONING TO OPEN THINKING and invite the construction of new connections and meanings.

QUESTIONING TO FOCUS THINKING and gently clarify ideas and increase precision.

EXTENDING thinking by providing resources and information.

PAUSING

There is a powerful connection between pausing and the quality and quantity of thinking that occurs in meetings. Unfortunately, in many working groups, pausing is an uncommon or underutilized resource. The pace of conversations affects both the emotional and intellectual climate for group members. For more introspective group members, fast-paced sessions may be oppressive or exclusionary. If group members with dispositions for thoughtfulness stop to reflect and ponder ideas or positions, the conversation often moves on without them. Conversations that shift quickly from idea-to-idea and person-to-person seem to assume a connection between speed and intelligence. Experienced and aware groups and experienced and aware facilitators come to realize that complex thinking takes and requires time.

Slowing down personal and group response times can feel uncomfortable at first. For most people, consciously pausing to provide a space for thinking requires patience, mindfulness and practice. Educator and researcher, Mary Budd Rowe (1986), defined three types of pausing or as she named it, wait time (see Table 2.3).

It is true I do not speak as well as I can think. But that is true of most people, as nearly as I can tell.
—Barbara Kingsolver,
The Poisonwood Bible

Wait Time I

Wait Time I is the length of time a facilitator or a group member waits after asking a question. Rowe suggested a 3–5 second pause to invite and ensure higher levels of thinking. This pause communicates a belief in group members' capacities for thought and reflection. It also increases processing time, so that more group members are likely to respond.

Wait Time II

Wait Time II is a pause after a response has been given. This pause provides time for thinkers to mentally retrieve additional and related information that extends the ideas presented in the initial response. A minimum of three seconds is recommended. More complex cognitive tasks may require five or more seconds to produce elaboration and clarification.

A facilitator's intention in learning-focused interactions should be to offer thought provoking paraphrases and thought provoking questions that invite participants to think deeply and diversely.

Table 2.3: Pausing to Enhance Thinking and Thoughtfulness

Wait Time I	Wait Time II	Wait Time III
Pause after asking a question	Pause after group members respond	Pause before your own responses or questions
• to allow thinking time	• to allow time for retrieval of additional and related information	• to model thoughtfulness and
• to signal support for thinking		• a need to think before responding
• to demonstrate your belief in group members' capacities for thinking		

By patiently providing quiet time for uninterrupted thinking, facilitators communicate this intention, crafting a container that supports community and cognition.

Wait Time III

Wait Time III is the pause that a facilitator or group member takes before responding to others. This pause communicates one's own need to craft thoughtful language; it models the importance of thinking before responding, and it displays a value for thoughtfulness. This pause may occur before any facilitator response. It often also occurs between the facilitator's paraphrase and his or her next question.

Explaining the usefulness of pausing is a group development resource. This strategy is particularly important to groups that are composed of noticeable extroverts and noticeable introverts. Without such cueing, extroverts tend to dominate and override the learning needs of quieter and more introspective colleagues. This approach also gives the facilitator permission to slow down processes by explicitly conveying the intentions of the pacing choices.

Facilitator modeling of the various types of pausing is the most effective teaching strategy for developing this resource within groups with which you work. It is worth the time and attention to over learn the patterns of pausing within the three types of wait time.

Anaviapik and the elders who came to visit him would often sit at his small kitchen table to exchange plans, reminisce, and tell stories. Whoever happened to be in the room would listen, punctuating what was said with questions and shouts of surprise. But those who listened did not interrupt with changes of topic or switch the conversation to themselves. A remarkable feature of Inuktitut, in fact, is the absence of devices for fending off possible interruption. There are no Inuktitut translations for 'er' and 'um.' The person who speaks can rely on speaking for as long as he or she wants. Oral cultures depend on respect, on allowing full space for people's words.   —Hugh Brody, The Other Side of Eden: Hunters, Farmers and the Shaping of the World

Paraphrasing to Establish Relationships, Increase Understanding and Mediate Thinking

Paraphrasing is one of the most valuable tools in a facilitator's and in an engaged group member's toolbox. Well-crafted paraphrases signal to others that they have our full attention. This skill requires listening at multiple levels and setting aside any chatter that might be rattling around in our own heads.

At the basic level, a paraphrase communicates that we understand others' thoughts, emotions, questions and ideas, or that we are attempting to do so. This signal that we are listening earns us psychological permission to inquire for the values, beliefs and assumptions behind the ideas of group members. It also earns us permission to inquire for details and press for elaboration of ideas, perceptions and proposals. Without a paraphrase, such inquiries may be perceived as an interrogation.

Thoughtfully designed paraphrases reduce the gap between speakers and responders, communicating a sense of regard and a desire to understand. Questions, however well intended and gently posed, are constructed from the inquirer's frame of reference, therefore creating distance.

Well-crafted paraphrases and appropriate pauses stimulate more thought than do questions alone. The pattern of pausing, paraphrasing and questioning supports relationship and learning. Mediational paraphrasing is a process organized by:

- An intention to support thinking and problem-solving.
- The attention of the paraphraser, who listens carefully for the essence of the message.
- The communication skills of the paraphraser.

Mediational paraphrases contain three essential elements; they label the speaker's *content*, they label the speaker's *emotions* about the content and they frame a *logical level* for holding that content (see Figure 2.2). Skilled paraphrasing treats responses as gifts. The paraphrase reflects a speaker's thinking providing opportunity for further consideration. In this way, the paraphrase connects the speaker and listener in a flow of discourse.

Figure 2.2: Template for Paraphrase

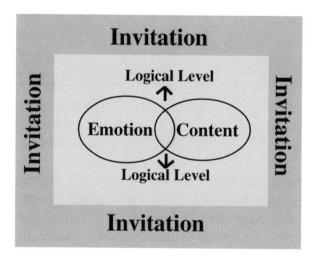

THREE INTENTIONS, THREE TYPES OF PARAPHRASES

Three types of paraphrases, with three different intentions, increase the range of possible responses. While each supports relationship and learning, paraphrases that shift the level of abstraction are more likely to create new levels of understanding. Paraphrases often move through a pattern of acknowledging and clarifying, then summarizing and organizing, then shifting the level of abstraction. However, there is no right sequence or formula for applying these responses. Cues from the speaker will help suggest the most appropriate form. Attentive facilitators and colleagues watch and listen for these cues, which include inflectional emphasis or repetition of certain words, often accompanied by gestures. Versatility in the use of paraphrase types gives skilled facilitators and skilled group members a wide range of actions from which to choose and an effective repertoire for supporting the growth of individuals and of groups as a whole.

Acknowledging and Clarifying

By restating the essence of another's statements, acknowledging and clarifying paraphrases provide opportunities to identify and calibrate content and emotions. Within their structure, they communicate a desire to understand ideas and they communicate our value for the speaker and what she or he is feeling and saying.

A Group Member Might Say	To Which A Facilitator or Another Group Member Might Respond:
"Many of these kids are not succeeding with this material."	"You're concerned about the performance levels of some of these students."
"This graph and data table are making me crazy, I can't make heads or tails out of it."	"This data set seems overwhelming at this point."

Effective acknowledging and clarifying paraphrases eliminate the personal pronouns I and me, as in "What *I* think *I* hear you saying is . . . " or "it seems to *me* that you are saying that . . ." Using these first person pronouns shifts the attention from the speaker to the paraphraser, which is not the intention of skillful paraphrasers. Further, such personal pronouns are statements of interpretation, not statements of reflection. While they are often intended as clarifications, there is a short distance between interpretation and judgment. An acknowledging and clarifying paraphrase packaged within an approachable voice encourages corrections or clarifying responses from the speaker, reinforcing his or her ownership of the conversation.

Summarizing and Organizing

Summarizing and organizing paraphrases offer themes and containers which shape initiating statements and separate jumbled issues. This type of paraphrase is especially useful in group work when there have been multiple speakers and a large volume of information shared.

Summarizing and organizing paraphrases capture key elements and offer organization to the initating statement, facilitating group reactions and responses. They provided shape and structure to conversations. These "shapes" include providing containers or categories.

	A Group Member Might Say	To Which A Facilitator or Another Group Member Might Respond
Containers	"I'm confused, the data seem to say that in language arts classes students are successfully participating in group activities, completing their assignments and transferring these learnings to independent work. In our math classes these same students are constantly off-task and require independent work assignments to keep control in the classroom."	"So, you're exploring two areas of student performance, language arts and math."
Comparisons and Contrasts	"This year's class is really struggling with problem-solving tasks. They're getting lost in the thinking and logical aspects and in the basic arithmetic."	"As you compare this year's group to last year's students you seem to be noticing some contrasts in their respective skill levels."
Sequence	"We need to get organized here. We've got a lot of work to do. We need to get inside this data set and the corresponding student work samples. We need to search for the most common mistakes, figure out why kids are making them and figure out what to do about all of this."	"You're proposing three tasks, first we'll examine the data and student work, then we'll sort by error type, and finally we'll craft intervention plans."

SHIFTING THE LEVEL OF ABSTRACTION

Shifting the level of abstraction is a paraphrase that moves language and thinking to a higher or lower logical level. The intention of this type of paraphrase is to illuminate large ideas or categories, which often leads speakers to new discoveries. When shifting down, this type of paraphrase focuses and clarifies, thereby increasing the precision of thinking.

For individuals and groups who think in highly sequential and concrete patterns, the shift up helps them to explore a bigger picture and provides a wider context for thought. For individuals and groups that tend to think in highly global patterns, the shift down grounds thinking in specific examples and concrete patterns.

We move to higher levels of thought and abstraction by naming big ideas, including concepts, categories, goals, and values.

	A Group Member Might Say	To Which A Facilitator or Another Group Member Might Respond
Goal	"These students are very needy and dependent on me for detailed directions at every turn."	"So, a goal for you might be to develop greater self-reliance in your learners."
Value	"Our program doesn't always challenge our most able students. They're sliding by and getting away with work that is not up to their full potential."	"So, you seem to value stretching high performing students and pushing them to increase their own expectations of themselves as learners."

A paraphrase that shifts to a higher level of abstraction is often particularly effective in problem-solving situations. Initially, more abstract language widens the potential solution set and encourages broader exploration of ideas and strategies for problem solving. For example, a group member might say: *"This multiple choice test doesn't measure my students' thinking ability."* To which a facilitator or another group member might respond: *"You're looking for assessment tools that provide a more authentic picture of your students' performance."*

We focus thinking by moving to lower levels of abstraction when ideas and concepts need grounding in details. We do so by offering specific details or examples within the paraphrase.

	A GROUP MEMBER MIGHT SAY	TO WHICH A FACILITATOR OR ANOTHER GROUP MEMBER MIGHT RESPOND
Strategy	"The school day is out of whack. Time blocks don't make sense for students or teachers. We're always rushing from one thing to another with no time to catch our breath or reflect."	"So, given those issues, this school might need to think about revising the yearly and daily schedules."
Action	"I think that some kids need to come to class regularly to succeed in school and some kids seem to be doing fine with independent projects and reading assignments."	"So, a first step might be to analyze attendance records for this class and compare them with performance results to determine what's best for each student."

A Scaffold for Crafting Paraphrases

Acknowledging and Clarifying	Summarizing and Organizing	Shifting Level of Abstraction
• *So, you're feeling* _____ • *You're noticing that* _____ • *In other words* _____ • *Hmm, you're suggesting that* _____	• *So, there seem to be two key issues here* _____ *and* _____. • *On the one hand there is* _____ *and on the other hand, there is* _____. • *It seems you're considering a sequence or hierarchy here; it might be* _____.	• *So a (n)* _____ *for you might be* _____. *(Shifting up) (Shifting down)* • *value* • *example* • *belief* • *non-example* • *assumption* • *strategy* • *goal* • *choice* • *intention* • *action* • *concept* • *option*

⭐ INTONATION MATTERS

Voice tone matters. The approachable voice, with its lilting cadence and upward ending inflection is an essential ingredient of successful paraphrases. This intonation pattern indicates your intention to check for accuracy in your paraphrase and invites correction, if needed. When a facilitator or group member uses a credible voice, which has a more modulated intonation ending in a downward tick, the paraphrases tends to sound presumptuous, as if he or she were reading the speaker's mind or telling them what they think. The approachable voice, with its rising inflection often motivates responses that are as thoughtful as the responses stimulated by well-crafted questions.

Timing is everything. Appropriately-timed paraphrases provide pivot points for shaping and shifting conversations. By acknowledging group members, summarizing the flow of the conversation, or shifting the level of abstraction up or down as needed, a facilitator can move the conversation through the paraphrase alone or redirect group attention with a targeted question. The facilitator's paraphrase provides a space for deciding the next move. Options include: paraphrase then question, paraphrase then give a direction, or paraphrase then offer information. Skillful facilitators artfully frame and energize dialogue and collaborative inquiry by using a pattern of pauses, paraphrases and questions that open or focus thinking.

In terms of group development, paraphrasing is a social resource. By subsuming the comments of all group members, including those without social or role status within summarizing and organizing paraphrases, skillful facilitators help their ideas be heard by others in the group. Such paraphrases subtly influence the sociology of a group. This is an especially useful approach for groups in which who says what carries more weight that what is being said.

TRY THIS

Paraphrasing works in concert with pausing and questioning to establish and support an environment for thinking. Review the following example. Then try the exercise to stretch your paraphrasing skills.

EXAMPLE

"Look at the data! The test scores across grades are all over the place and they have been declining steadily for the past four years for some of these kids!"

ACKNOWLEDGING AND CLARIFYING	SUMMARIZING AND ORGANIZING	SHIFTING THE LEVEL OF ABSTRACTION
"You're concerned about these patterns of student performance."	"There seem to be two trends here—erratic grade level scores and a decline for certain populations."	"So, a goal might be to consistently improve performance for all grade levels and all students."

PRACTICE SAMPLE

"It's been really tough this year. The expectations are increasing while the resources are shrinking. And now we have all this assessment and reporting to do."

ACKNOWLEDGING AND CLARIFYING	SUMMARIZING AND ORGANIZING	SHIFTING THE LEVEL OF ABSTRACTION

MEDIATIONAL QUESTIONS

Expert facilitators craft mediational questions that open group members' thinking and mediational questions that focus group members' thinking (see Figure 2.3). This strategic repertoire joins pausing and paraphrasing within a facilitator's toolbox to engage, energize and organize the thought processes of working groups. This same tool set applied by group members as agents of growth empowers groups to explore ideas, analyze data of all types and develop options for improvement.

Figure 2.3: Mediational Questions

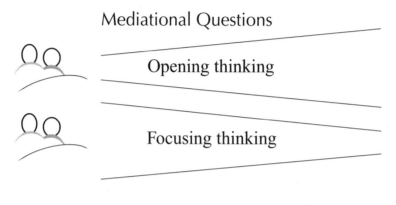

QUESTIONS THAT OPEN THINKING

Questions that open and illuminate thinking invite a wide range of potential responses. Language and thinking once surfaced, can then be honed and refined. But until thinking emerges within the group, there is little with which to work. The intention of inquiry is to support group members in exploring ideas, issues, concerns, perspectives and proposals. Like the paraphrase, well-crafted inquiries integrate three essential elements: an *invitation* to engage and think, a *cognitive focus* for thinking about the topic and a *topic* to think about (see Figure 2.4).

Figure 2.4: Three Essential Elements

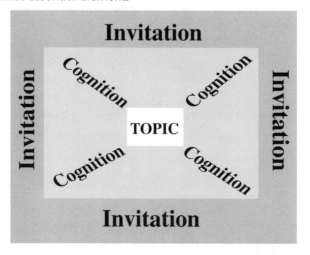

These elements may be combined in a variety of combinations and do not always appear in the same order within a question. Personal style and context influence question construction.

When our goal is to promote higher levels of thinking, packaging our questions within the invitational elements introduced earlier in this chapter matters greatly. These physical, tonal and linguistic layers reduce any potential threats within our inquiries, making it emotionally and intellectually easier for group members to engage with the question and the questioner. By embedding plural forms and exploratory language, we open up a greater palate of possibilities for perspective seeking, exploration and idea generation. The questions within the Collaborative Learning Cycle reflect these invitational qualities and the open-ended, nondichotomous intention of such questions.

The various stages of collaborative inquiry and data-driven dialogue require specific types of thinking. Learning-focused facilitators construct mediational questions that are purposefully driven by cognitive intentions. For example, the phases of the Collaborative Learning Cycle each have a specific cognitive focus (see Table 2.4). Activating and engaging prior knowledge requires recalling, speculating, predicting, and assuming. Exploring and discovering with data requires: observing, analyzing, comparing, contrasting, and relating. Organizing and integrating requires: inferring, evaluating, generalizing, and theorizing. Mediational questions that invite and open thinking build collaborative capacities, expand the possibilities and promote ownership of ideas and actions.

You see, I am not asking another question each time. I am making the same question bigger.
—*Gregory Bateson*

Table 2.4: Cognitive Operations

ACTIVATING AND ENGAGING	EXPLORING AND DISCOVERING	ORGANIZING AND INTEGRATING
• recall	• observe	• infer
• estimate	• describe	• evaluate
• speculate	• sort	• classify
• predict	• analyze	• interpret
• assume	• relate	• summarize
• visualize	• compare	• generalize
• wonder	• contrast	• theorize
• forecast	• distinguish	• hypothesize

Skilled facilitators and group members assemble questions by combining the various linguistic elements to form language that opens thinking. Use the following syntactical elements to construct samples of mediational questions. Each question should have an *invitational element,* a *cognitive focus* and a *topic.*

INVITATIONAL STEMS	COGNITIVE FOCUS	TOPICS
What are some . . .	predict	student work
What seems . . .	assume	survey results
What are your hunches about . . .	analyze	observations
What are some possible . . .	compare	test scores
How might these . . .	interpret	work samples
What is your sense of . . .	generalize	data

EXAMPLES:

1. *What are some* of your *assumptions* about how the *survey results* will vary by grade level?
    Invitation —what are some
    Cognition—assumptions
    Topic—survey results

2. *Compare* this year's *results* with your goals for your students, *what are some possible* factors that influenced these outcomes?
    Cognition—compare
    Topic—results
    Invitation—what are some possible

    Experiment by varying the syntax, adding prefaces such as: *as you...given these... considering these...based on . . .*

3. As you interpret these test scores, what are some of the things that you are noticing?

4. Given your generalizations about these student work samples, what seems most important to you at this point?

5. Considering your analysis of this data set, what are some of the things that you are noticing?

6. Based on your inferences about this student's performance, what are some possible elements we might consider?

TRY THIS

PRACTICE SAMPLES

Craft three mediational questions of your own. Develop as much variety as you can between your samples. Please feel free to add your own topics and to draw from the greater list of cognitive operations found on page 31.

QUESTIONS THAT FOCUS THINKING

Language is a trap door that often obscures or hides what resides beneath it. All language has deeper attached meanings. The person speaking the words knows some of these meanings but some of these meanings remain hidden until teased into view.

Words are navigational markers to the map of our world. These maps are functional approximations of reality. They provide points of reference and directional cues from which we shape our choices and behaviors. Yet for all of us, the maps are incomplete. Our brains are not genetically designed to operate with a complete and accurate set of details. Human brains evolved to organize useful levels of generalization that shape and guide our thinking and actions. Human language reflects these thinking habits, producing surface vagueness that often masks the rich details that lie beneath. Our brains create and are created by models of the reality emerging from our experiences. We delete and distort incoming and outgoing data to fit these embedded filters (Bandler and Grinder, 1971).

The brain and nervous system also have built-in circuits for forgetting. Without this, we would soon overload the system. Imagine what life would be like if we remembered every face and every conversation we encountered in a day, a week, or a month. Our world floods us with irrelevant information, which is soon discarded from the files of working memory.

As human beings and human brains evolved, generalizations, deletions and distortions in thinking and in language served our hunting and gathering ancestors well as they made the quick decisions necessary for survival. These same thinking and language attributes become barriers in contemporary human communication. One important way that facilitators and group members make a difference for their colleagues is by supporting precision in thinking. By identifying and clarifying specifics, alert facilitators and aware participants can help shift situations that might feel overwhelming to the group to ones that are more manageable emotionally, mentally and physically. Like many mediative skills, questions that focus thinking are based on listening. In this case, listening for vague language and deciding which terms, if clarified, might enhance communication, ground the conversation and support the most productive shifts in thinking.

Vague thinking and vague language patterns occur within five major categories (Laborde, 1984). These categories become listening lenses for attuned facilitators and group members who then select a focus for clarification, paraphrase the essential ideas and ask questions to clarify these areas of imprecision. In many cases, more than one category of vagueness appears in the same statement.

VAGUE NOUNS AND PRONOUNS. Vague nouns and pronouns occur commonly in everyday language. In schools we hear about, my students, the test scores, that class, my fourth period group, the curriculum, student behaviors, parents, the central office, and a host of other unspecified nouns and pronouns. For many educators, someone named "they" causes most of the problems in their class, school or district. We, us and them are additional sources of concern or joy.

In meetings we might hear a participant say, "Our students' work shows that they don't understand fractions and decimals." If we wish to move ahead with this conversation, we need to clarify how many students don't understand these elements of mathematics and which parts of fractions and decimals seem most confusing. Without these essential details, other group members don't know where to target their energy and attention within the problem-solving conversation. By sorting and narrowing the field of focus, the group can identify specific groups of learners and better identify their precise learning needs.

VAGUE VERBS. The verb understand in the example above is another critical variable to sort out within this problem-solving process. What might students be saying and doing when they understand fractions and decimals? Problem finding, data analysis, planning and decision making all require specificity to focus understanding and actions.

Planning and goal setting are fertile areas for asking questions that focus the thinking of group members. Words like, plan, improve, design, modify, enhance, and prepare are all examples of vague verbs that have little meaning without clarification and defined actions.

COMPARATORS. There are two primary types of vagueness relating to comparators: the criteria for comparison and the source of comparison. When a group member says, "This meeting was better than last week's session," two queries might be productive avenues to explore. One is, "In what ways was it better?" and the other is, "What was it better than?" Until the group knows the speaker's criteria for "better" it does not know how to proceed with the conversation. Is this "better" a success to build upon or are there poorly understood factors at work here that leave this "better" a mystery for all to ponder? Other vague comparators are words like best, larger, slower, more, less and least.

Facilitators and group member support their colleagues by helping them specify their standards and criteria for comparison. This action develops clarity in problem analysis, planning, and implementation, driven by targeted action and measurable signs of success. When a meeting participant says, "I want our students to get better results on the next assessment," the facilitator or another group member might respond by framing a question that would help the speaker define the qualities of better results. Does the speaker mean a higher class average, a narrower gap between high and low performers, fewer students below standard or some other improvement criteria? The group also needs to surface the lost comparator, which is the previous exam. How well did students do in that instance? What target areas emerged from consideration of this prior performance? Without clarifying these details, the conversation is potentially ungrounded, unproductive and built on individual impressions.

RULE WORDS. We all have sets of rules that guide our way of perceiving and operating in the world. Humans are not always conscious of these internal codes, yet they appear in our language when we say things like. "I have to", "I must", "I can't" and "I shouldn't have." Working groups, like individuals, share tacit rules. In the examples above, the pronoun we can be easily substituted for the pronoun I.

When a facilitator or group member hears a participant speak a phrase like the ones above, it may be appropriate to check for the rule behind the statement. "When you say that 'you have to', who says you have to?" "What would happen if you didn't?" "What stops you from doing that?"

Intonation matters greatly here. The facilitator's voice must be carefully modulated and approachable to create a safe environment for exploring the internal rules governing the external language.

UNIVERSAL QUANTIFIERS. "All the parents in the school are upset about the new reporting system." "Our students always get confused with those types of exam questions." Linguists label words and phrases like everyone, all, no one, never, and always as universal quantifiers. They also use the term deity voice to label this type of language because these terms are spoken as if the statement possesses a universal truth understood by everyone.

By clarifying the universal quantifier, a facilitator or skilled group member helps other participants ground the conversation with measurable details and supportable data. When a participant says, "These kids are never here on time," the facilitator might respond, "Never? Has there ever been an instance when most of them were on time?"

Vague Language
- *Nouns and Pronouns*
- *Verbs*
- *Comparators*
- *Rule Words*
- *Universal Quantifiers*

TRY THIS

Review the following examples. Identify the vague language. How might you clarify these statements?

- These performance data never make any sense.

- Parents don't care about school success.

- Our students always do well with those types of questions.

- We're not ready to take that on.

- We have to do it this way.

- This seminar is better.

⛤ LEARNING TO LISTEN FOR VAGUENESS

Learning to listen for vague language is a useful facilitation skill. Like many such skills it is important to over learn this tool so that it is easily accessible, requiring minimal mental energy when you are facilitating a session. There are several practical ways to internalize this type of listening. One is to script examples during meetings in which you are a participant and practice asking clarifying questions. Another is to search for advertisements that purposely use vague language in their enticements. An additional approach is to script interviews broadcast on radio and television.

PATTERNS OF INQUIRY

Questions that open and questions that focus may be perceived as intrusive or as interrogations if they are not preceded by thoughtful paraphrases. The pattern of pausing, paraphrasing and questioning to focus thinking communicates an intention to understand the speaker and an intention to support clarity and deeper thinking.

Timing and attention to the effects of one's actions is critical to these processes. If information or approaches are shared too early in a session, group members may get the impression that the facilitator thinks that they are not capable of independent thinking and decision making. If a facilitator waits too long before intervening, and frustration sets in, group members may be unduly stressed. Our choice of action needs to align with our intentions to extend thinking and to support the relationship with and within the group.

EXTENDING THINKING

A facilitator's knowledge and resource banks establish a rich basis for supporting the thinking and problem-solving of others. Facilitators extend the thinking of group members by supplying additional information, framing clear expectations for outcomes and processes, and directing others to essential professional resources. These resources might include other professionals in the district, print and audiovisual materials, or technology-based information such as pertinent websites. Such resources might also come in the form of demonstrations using data analysis tools or graphic planning tools such as the Interrelationship Diagram described in Chapter Five.

BALANCING ADVOCACY AND INQUIRY

Successful data-driven dialogue requires individuals to carefully balance advocacy for their own ideas and viewpoints with equal amounts of time and energy focused on inquiring into the positions and viewpoints of others. This ability involves emotional, cognitive, attentive and linguistic resources (see Table 2.5).

The goal is to make the thinking of all group members explicit and open to shared examination. In the process, frames of reference and

From Inquiry to Advocacy Transition Stems

- *My thoughts on that include . . .*
- *From my perspective, we could . . .*
- *A related idea might be . . .*
- *I think about it slightly differently . . .*
- *Another way to think about that might be . . .*

operating assumptions move to the surface where they can be explored, clarified, modified, and potentially owned by the group. Peter Senge (1990) calls this process reciprocal inquiry. Advocacy is well served by embedding positive presuppositions within your statements of assumption. For example, "Given our focus on improving the writing skills of all of our students, my assumption is that we should include the special education teachers in the planning process."

When group members embrace this intention, they move from attempting to "win" the argument to a desire to find the best argument with the most compelling data to support that position. When we attempt to win, we tend to use data selectively to confirm our position. By balancing our advocacy with inquiry into the ideas of others, we open ourselves and the group to the power of disconfirming and discomforting data. This individual and collective rethinking opens possibilities for fresh perspectives and novel approaches to problems.

Table 2.5: Skilled Advocacy

IS . . .	IS NOT . . .
stating assumptions	declaring passions
describing reasoning	staking of positions
describing feelings	getting lost in emotions
distinguishing data from interpretations	making generalizations from little data
revealing perspectives	assuming there is only one viewpoint
framing issues in wider contexts	getting lost in details
giving concrete examples	avoiding the practical
offering points of confusion	confusing confidence with clarity

Adapted from Ross and Roberts, 1994

I believe in all that has not yet been spoken.

—*Rainer Maria Rilke*

The Book of Hours: Love Poems to God

DIALOGUE

Dialogue is one of the most ancient forms of human communication. Our tribal ancestors gathered around their fires crafting humanity and community with stories, songs and conversations. By learning the processes of dialogue we restore the patterns of our elders and embrace habits still practiced by indigenous peoples across the planet.

Many of these communication and thinking patterns were set aside during the development of western culture as the early Greek philosophers and later European thinkers shaped language and listening models for logic, reasoning and persuading. These habits of mind molded our culture as we now know and experience it, producing the technological, social and political structures that make us who we are today.

By embracing the processes and patterns of dialogue we do not deny other ways of interacting. Dialogue is an important addition to individual and group repertoire. It extends personal and collaborative capabilities by supporting speaking and listening behaviors that link people and ideas. This collective search seeks connections, not fissures, and wholes, not parts. At the most fundamental level, dialogue is a process of listening and speaking to understand each other's ideas, assumptions, beliefs and values. To understand others does not imply agreement or disagreement with their viewpoints. Dialogue seeks and explores the layers of meaning within ideas.

The physicist, David Bohm, brought consciousness to dialogue in its more modern form, promoting it as an intentional communication process to develop deeper forms of collective thinking. He combined knowledge of quantum physics with understandings influenced by his work and association with the Indian philosopher, Jiddu Krishnamurti. Bohm sought patterns of thought in individuals and patterns of thought in society. From his studies with Krishnamurti, he learned the value of observing his own internal stream of consciousness and extended this to the value of observing the ways in which collective thought unfolds during purposeful conversations.

"Dialogue comes from the Greek word dialogos. Logos means 'the word', or in our case we would think of the 'meaning of the word'. And dia means 'through'—it doesn't mean two. A dialogue can be among any number of people, not just two. Even one person can have a sense of dialogue within himself, if the spirit of dialogue is present. The picture or image that this derivation suggests is of a stream of meaning flowing among and through us and between us. This will make possible a flow of meaning in the whole group, out of which will emerge some new understanding. It's something new, which may not have been in the starting point at all. It is something creative. And this shared meaning is the 'glue' or 'cement' that holds people and societies together."

—David Bohm

On Dialogue

Bohm's work in turn influenced the work of William Isaacs, and his colleague, Peter Senge, at the MIT Center for Organizational Learning. Isaacs (1999) calls dialogue a conversation with a center, not sides. It requires a full commitment as a listener to understand others and a full commitment as a speaker to be understood by others. Like a magnetic field, the practice of dialogue gives a shape and structure to a spirit of sustained collective inquiry within and between people.

Within this container, we find the psychological safety to talk about the hard to talk about things that matter. To craft this container requires a blend of internal and external quiet so we can hear ourselves, hear others and hear ourselves hear others. "Our conversations organize the processes and structures which shape our collective future" (Isaacs, 1999, p. xi). This thinking together, in itself, is a value and an outcome. The process is also the product.

Dialogue is an adaptive force when used within groups and organizations. The practice of dialogue develops self-organizing systems that clarify and maintain core identities. Given the nonlinear nature of systems and the forces around systems, planned actions and interactions are often difficult to predict with clarity and confidence. Dialogue helps us to find connection and meaning within the noise.

SKILLED DISCUSSION

Skilled discussion couples with skilled dialogue to support clarity of thought and commitment to action. For discussions to be productive, group members and groups need to be clear about the purpose of their interactions. While dialogue is about open exploration of ideas and perspectives, skilled discussion seeks focus and closure on a set of actions. This process, in turn, requires group members to balance advocacy for their ideas with equal energy inquiring into the ideas of others. Skilled discussion also depends upon healthy norms of critical thinking to allow groups to sort and analyze data, information and proposals. Lastly, skilled discussion is not possible without group member clarity about the decision-making processes that will focus actions and the implications and consequences of those decisions.

Data-driven dialogue and data-driven discussions have much in common. They each require the full attention of participants, careful listening, linguistic skills and the intention to separate data and facts from inference and opinions. The defining characteristics of each are in Table 2.6.

DATA-DRIVEN DIALOGUE VERSUS DATA-BASED DECISIONS

Dialogue that leads to collaborative planning and problem solving is not the same as what is commonly presented as data-based decision-making. Data-based decision making does not always assume collective processes. Leaders and specialists often analyze data sets and then attempt to explain what the numbers mean to others who must first own the problem before they can move towards solutions. In the worst cases, decisions about such things as curriculum, instruction,

Table 2.6: Dialogue and Discussion

DIALOGUE	DISCUSSION
thinking holistically	thinking analytically
making connections	making distinctions
surfacing and inquiring into assumptions	surfacing and inquiring into assumptions
developing shared meaning	developing agreement on action
seeking understanding	seeking decisions

scheduling, and student groupings are imposed upon people who do not yet understand the underlying problems such innovations attempt to solve. In some settings, well intended processes short circuit when groups lack maps and tools for collaborative inquiry, problem-solving and planning.

In contrast, data-driven dialogue is a collective process designed to create shared understandings of issues and events using information from many different sources. Well-crafted dialogue honors the emotional as well as the rational components of problem-finding and problem solving. The processes of data-driven dialogue both require and develop changes in the working culture of many groups and many organizations. It separates inquiry, analysis and problem finding from the rush to decide and the rush to act.

In too many schools we find groups lurching from problems to programs as they seek the comfort of action over the discomfort and the messiness of collaborative inquiry and investigation of root causes. Data-driven dialogue presses the pause button, inviting group members to reflect and inspect current results arising from current practices and beliefs about learning, teaching and engaging in common cause.

In the next chapter we present a model for structuring and guiding collaborative inquiry—data-driven dialogue. The model applies to group work with all types of data, from student work samples to teacher made tests to criterion-referenced and nationally-normed examinations.

Notes

CHAPTER THREE—A Model for Collaborative Inquiry: How We Talk

"People who have developed expertise in particular areas are, by definition, able to think effectively about problems in those areas. Understanding expertise is important because it provides insights into the nature of thinking and problem solving. Research shows that it is not simply general abilities such as memory or intelligence, nor the use of general strategies that differentiate experts from novices. Instead, experts have acquired extensive knowledge that affects what they notice and how they organize, represent, and interpret information in their environment. This, in turn, affects their abilities to remember, reason and solve problems."

—Bransford, Brown and Cocking

Groups, both small and large, need templates to guide purposeful inquiry. No matter the degree of comfort that any individual within the group has with data, collective focus is often difficult when there is no shape to the conversation.

The Collaborative Learning Cycle described in this chapter frames data exploration as a learning process. It is an adaptation of the three-phase Pathways Learning Model (Lipton and Wellman, 2000) that is steeped in current understandings about how we learn. Each phase of the model promotes specific types of thinking and interactions. The framework supports a learning environment in which participant engagement with information and fellow learners ignites the processes of inquiry and problem solving. The model draws upon current thinking in the field of cognitive psychology, social psychology and instructional design. This model is illustrated here as a question-driven design for inquiring into data (see Figure 3.1).

The first phase, Activating and Engaging, brings learners and their prior experiences metaphorically and physically to the table. The second phase, Exploring and Discovering, structures focused inquiry into data, connecting it to prior experience and setting the scene for theory building. The third phase, Organizing and Integrating, develops confidence in theories of causation for the issues and problems under study, and confidence and commitment to theories of action for addressing them.

The model reflects the integrity of these three distinct phases of inquiry into data, providing the foundation for careful problem solving,

Figure 3.1: The Collaborative Learning Cycle

The Collaborative Learning Cycle

Organizing Dialogue for Connection Making

Activating and Engaging

Surfacing experiences and expectations

What are some predictions we are making?
With what assumptions are we entering?
What are some questions we are asking?
What are some possibilities for learning that
   this experience presents to us?

Organizing and Integrating

Generating theory

What inferences / explanations / conclusions
   might we draw? (causation)
What additional data sources might we explore
   to verify our explanations? (confirmation)

What are some solutions we might explore
   as a result of our conclusions? (action)
What data will we need to collect to guide
   implementation? (calibration)

Managing
Modeling
Mediating
Monitoring

Exploring and Discovering

Analyzing the data

What important points seem to "pop-out"?
What are some patterns, categories or trends
   that are emerging?
What seems to be surprising or unexpected?
What are some things we have not yet explored?

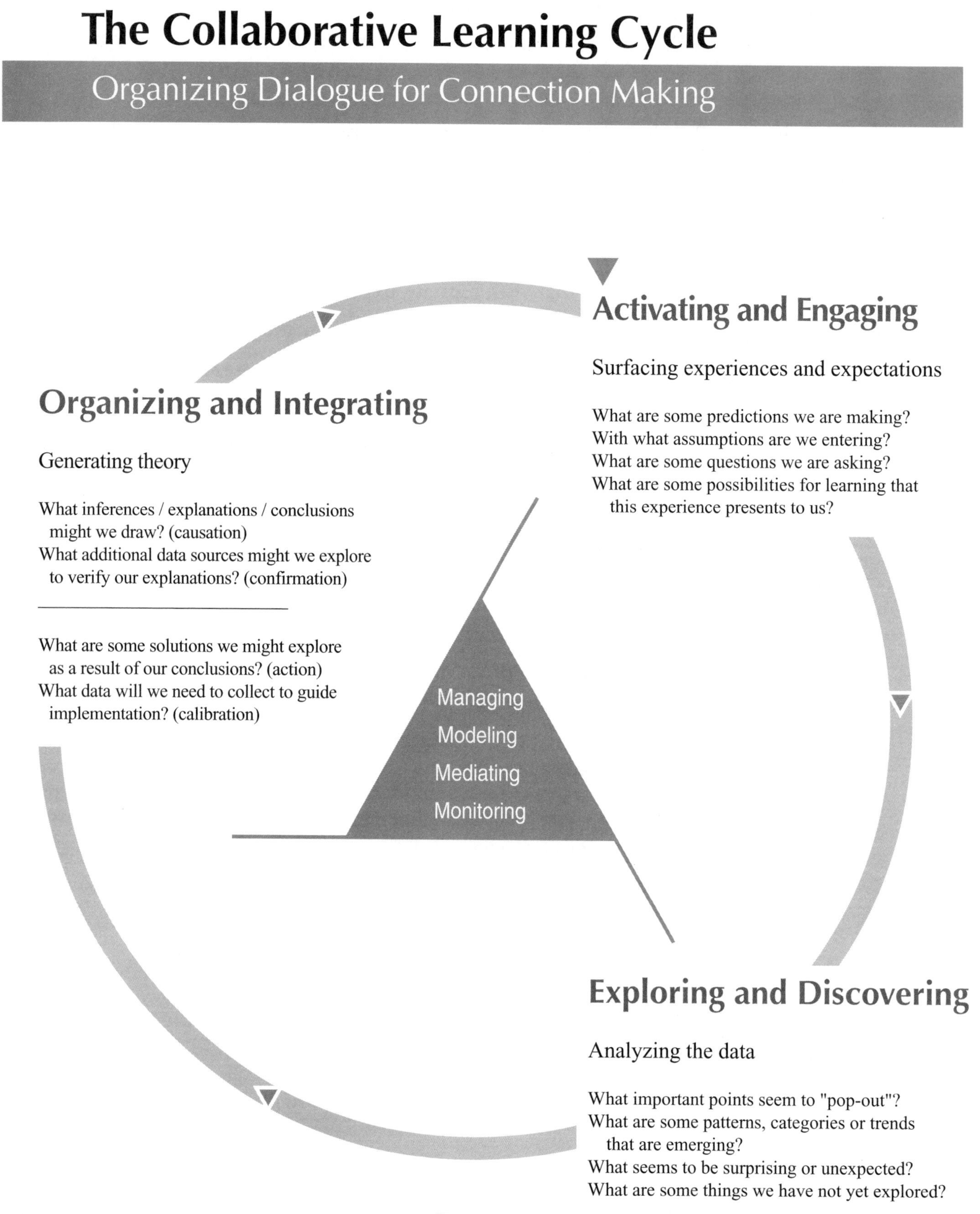

planning, experimentation and implementation. The guiding questions within each phase shape the cognitive and affective intentions of that aspect of the inquiry. Each phase presents rich possibilities and with effective implementation, avoids critical liabilities. With mindful facilitation, the Collaborative Learning Cycle honors and satisfies the three functions of group development presented in the previous chapter: attending to task, attending to process, and attending to relationship.

ACTIVATING AND ENGAGING: SURFACING EXPERIENCES AND EXPECTATIONS

This phase occurs without the data being present. It sets the tone, establishes group norms and shapes expectations for how the exploration of the data will occur. This is true whether the data to be examined is from "official" state, provincial or local tests, classroom work samples, or survey and opinion sources.

POSSIBILITIES

Activating and engaging prior knowledge honors and expands group members' expertise and experience and develops readiness for exploring and discovering within the data set during the following phase. Predicting activities surface areas of expectation, anticipation, and curiosity. This first phase allows and encourages participants to share what they think they will see in the data set and why they think that might be so. By surfacing predictions and assumptions, groups and group members name the frames of reference that are the lenses through which they view the world. These same lenses are also the frames through which individuals and groups view any data that are before them. Naming and exploring these assumptions before the data are present open possibilities for reframing and rethinking habits of mind that tacitly and overtly guide instructional decision-making and teaching practices.

SEPARATE PREDICTIONS FROM ASSUMPTIONS

Some groups and group members have difficulty separating predictions from assumptions. Listen carefully to statements of prediction and note whether these are predictions or are in fact assumptions. Inquire into the statement to surface and separate assumptions that may be underlying stated predictions.

Distinguishing between assumptions and predictions is essential for building shared understandings, seeing new possibilities, framing problems and defining solutions. For example, in one group with which we were about to examine some grade five math data, a participant made the statement that the girls would out perform the boys on this standards-based assessment. On the surface, this is a prediction. Left unsaid was an assumption that the girls had better reading skills and better work habits which would influence performance on a math exam that emphasized word problems. If the prediction remained unexamined, the chain of logic embedded in the assumption would have been invisible to the rest of the group (and even to the specific participant). Surfacing the assumption opened up a productive dialogue about gender differences in math learning, the nature of the math standards, and clarification of technical features of the test.

Skilled facilitators purposefully activate the necessary cognitive and emotional resources needed for the task before the group. These might include such dispositions as open-mindedness, willingness to listen to other perspectives, and confidence in the collective ability of the group to productively solve important instructional problems. This type of activating is especially important when individual group members are familiar with the data that is to be collaboratively explored. Several of the tools in Chapter Five serve these purposes, including: Synectics—Four-Box; Round the Room and Back Again; and Brainstorm and Pass.

LIABILITIES

When groups skip the Activating and Engaging phase, members can get lost in the sea of data and opinions. They do not know what to expect from the data and from each other. They sometimes enter with defensive postures, ready to attack, or deny what appears before them. Many groups overlook the importance of activating and engaging and are later surprised when there are wide discrepancies in individual perceptions about the data being examined.

EXPLORING AND DISCOVERING: ANALYZING THE DATA

This phase is the heart of collaborative inquiry. Group members require mental and emotional discipline to work productively with the data and with each other. Collective understanding that merges the best of multiple perspectives is the goal. This outcome means that both the data literate and the data shy have their own challenges. The data literate often need to refrain from dominating the group and explaining what the data mean. The data shy often need encouragement and the courage to ask what they fear might be obvious questions about what the data mean or how to read the data displays. They also might be reluctant to share their ideas regarding what the data reflect about student performance.

DEPERSONALIZE THE DATA

Depersonalizing the data makes it emotionally easier for groups to explore and discover. Use impersonal pronouns to reference the data. Instead of saying, "What does this graph say about 'our' (teaching, curriculum, program etc.)?" ask "What pops out?" or "What are some of the patterns here?" The intention is to turn the data into a thing that can be discussed with less emotion than if the display is viewed as a mirror of personal performance.

Data-Driven Dialogue

- *Conscious Curiosity*
- *Purposeful Uncertainty*
- *Visually Vibrant Information*

POSSIBILITIES

Two habits of mind, conscious curiosity and purposeful uncertainty, guide this phase. To explore and discover, groups must avoid rushing to premature conclusions. To remain open to possibilities and fresh ways of framing problems, they must stay with the data and push themselves to explore multiple story lines within it. This is a phase of distinguishing, sorting, analyzing, comparing, and contrasting. It is not a phase of explaining. The word "because" undermines this type of thinking. As soon as group members start explaining why the data look as they do, they tend to quit exploring and lock into biased descriptions and premature explanations for both high and low performance.

Visually vibrant displays support group exploration of data (Tufte, 1983). In our experience, large shared data displays are far superior to individual data sheets. Shared displays focus group attention on one point of interest at a time. Group members then have a collaborative learning experience instead of dropping individually into charts and graphs seeking separate points of information (see more on data display in Chapter Four: A Data Primer).

LIABILITIES

Poorly structured versions of the Exploring and Discovering phase are a primary source of difficulty in data-based processes. Cluttered or overwhelming data displays confuse groups, which must spend much of their time and energy trying to sort out critical details. Data sets are always incomplete. For example, norm referenced math and reading scores only tell part of the story. Nevertheless, groups often limit their exploration, relying on too little information and developing premature solutions for ill-defined problems. Exploration then disintegrates into explanation.

Faced with the choice between changing one's mind and proving that there is no need to do so, almost everybody gets busy on the proof.

—John Kenneth Galbraith

Intellectual Hangtime

Bob Gore, former CEO of W.L. Gore & Associates, the manufacturers of such products as Gore-tex® fabrics and Glide Dental Floss®, is renowned among his managers and employees for his ability to ask insightful questions that reframe thinking. He systematically avoids the rush to closure, seeking fresh perspectives for problems and approaches. His colleagues refer to this as "intellectual hangtime," likening this emotional and cognitive ability to the hangtime of gifted basketball players who seem to suspend themselves in air as they search for an opening to the basket.   *—Michael Pacanowsky*

ORGANIZING AND INTEGRATING: GENERATING THEORY

This third phase of the Collaborative Learning Cycle organizes the transition to formal problem finding and problem solving setting the scene for detailed planning processes. Facilitators must take care at this phase to help groups stay open to multiple interpretations of why the data look as they do. Multiple voices and multiple perspectives serve the work at this stage. Groups usually come to realize that the data before them do not tell the whole story and that they need more information to increase their confidence in any explanation of why things appear as they do.

Theory is a necessary myth that we construct to understand something we know we understand incompletely. Theory is a deliberate attempt to go beyond what we know or to correct what we think are the erroneous explanations of others. It is intended to make a difference not only on the level of theory but on the level of action, be it in a laboratory, a classroom, or a school.

—Seymour B. Sarason

POSSIBILITIES

Organizing and Integrating has two essential components: framing the problem and developing solutions. Skillful facilitation and productive inquiry separates the generation of theories of causation from the generation of theories of action. This concept is graphically illustrated by the dividing line in the Organizing and Integrating phase of the Collaborative Learning Cycle (see Figure 3.2). For example, a data display showing student performance in middle school mathematics will show both high and low performance at a typical grade level. Potential causes across the performance continuum are multiple and varied, and might include instructional methods, teacher content expertise, curriculum and materials, community expectations and time allotments. Skillful groups develop multiple theories of causation before they attempt to generate theories of action. They search for possible stories within the data. In this way, groups widen the story line seeking new perspectives.

Figure 3.2: Organizing and Integrating

Organizing and Integrating

Generating theory

What inferences / explanations / conclusions might we draw? (causation)
What additional data sources might we explore to verify our explanations? (confirmation)

What are some solutions we might explore as a result of our conclusions? (action)
What data will we need to collect to guide implementation? (calibration)

SEEK MULTIPLE INTERPRETATIONS

Help groups avoid the temptation to come to premature closure. Request at least three potential theories of causation, and structure an examination of each before moving on to theories of action.

This phase of the model calls for generating several likely causes, based on the interpretation of the data. This process leads to identifying additional data sources to confirm and clarify emerging causal theories. Increasing confidence in the most likely causal theories develops as a result of the group's thoughtful analysis of this new information. Only then, can and should groups consider theories of action.

Theories of action lead to problem solving, planning, and action research projects guided by the ongoing use of formal and informal data, thus continuing the learning cycle started by a given round of data-driven collaborative inquiry.

Word Source

The words theory and theater share the same Greek root, 'theoros' which means a way of viewing. When we go to the theater, the space and the production design—the lighting, the sound and the staging—shape a way of viewing for the audience. We experience and interpret the story presented through this frame. Our theories have the same effect on our perceptions of the world around us; they frame the stories that we tell and our interpretation of the stories that others tell.

LIABILITIES

Rapid closure on one theory of action is the enemy at this stage. In the press of time, any action is sought over further reflection. Theories of action override theories of causation. Herbert Simon, a Nobel laureate in economics, noted this tendency in decision-making groups. He coined the terms *bounded rationality* and *satisficing* to describe these behaviors (Beach, 1997).

Herbert Simon used the metaphor of a pair of scissors to describe the limitations within decision making processes. One scissor blade is the cognitive abilities of individuals and the collective reasoning abilities of groups. The other blade is the structure of the environment within which a group operates. The environment includes both the external social, cultural and political context within which a group operates and the internal social, cultural and political context of the group itself.

Working groups of decision-makers have a limited cognitive capacity for holding complexity so they try to simplify problems to more limited or bounded versions. In this way, they reduce the information-processing load. Satisficing means an idea or intended action is minimally satisfying and minimally sufficient for addressing an issue or problem. Operationally, this tendency causes groups to jump to the first option they've developed that seems to fit the bounded version of the problem.

In Herbert Simon's view, decision making is a search process guided by aspiration levels. That is, groups decide, either explicitly or by tacit

Research is formalized curiosity. It is poking and prying with purpose. It is a seeking that he who wishes may know the cosmic secrets of the world and they that dwell therein.

—Zora Neal Hurston

The final conclusion is that we know very little, and yet it is astounding that we know so much, and still more astounding that so little knowledge can give us so much power.

—Bertrand Russell

agreement how ambitious or complex a goal they are willing to pursue. A search process goes on until satisficient alternatives emerge that meet the aspiration levels of the goals a group is pursuing (Selten, 2001). Aspiration levels are not permanently fixed. Groups adjust them to a given situation and to different contexts. Aspiration levels can make groups self-limiting or expanding in their pursuit of problem-solving.

One goal of group development, and what may be the truest test of professional community in schools, is the adjustment of the aspiration levels of goals for improving student learning. As colleagues develop expanded confidence in their own capacities and in the capacities of others, their willingness to persevere with problem finding and problem solving increases. An example of this dynamic occurs when groups take on improvements in student reading performance. If political pressures demand immediate result, groups often focus their energy on those students who are just below the cut off point that determines proficiency. As more and more students meet this challenge, teacher teams then start to look more closely at other measures of reading success and ratchet up their expectations for all learners. In this way, they adjust their aspirations and set more ambitious goals for themselves and their students.

Ultimately, a cycle develops within the bounded frame of group processing; problem framing leads to a search for alternatives guided by data; the group makes satisficient selections from the options and adapts its aspiration levels in response to environmental conditions. As aspiration levels shift, new problems emerge, leading to new data searches, additional decisions, continued exploration and growth.

PLAN TIME WISELY

Given the realities of time constraints, it may be useful to address the three phases in separate sessions. For example, a meeting focused on Activating and Engaging prepares a group emotionally and cognitively for exploring data sets and displays, which may be developed in separate sessions by technical resource staff. Exploring and Discovering and the first phase of Organizing and Integrating (developing theories of causation) function effectively together in a subsequent session. Once a group gathers confirming data for its theories of causation, it can then segue into developing theories of action and formal planning processes in a final session.

DATA-DRIVEN LEARNING

When groups employ structural scaffolds, such as the Collaborative Learning Cycle, to guide and facilitate their developing skillfulness, they increase their confidence and success in working with data and with working with each other.

As we learn to link statistics and stories, numbers and narrative and data and dialogue, new possibilities for community building and richer forms of professional practice emerge that will better serve student learning in these changing times.

CHAPTER FOUR—A Data Primer

da·ta: *noun; plural, but singular or plural in construction,* from the Latin, plural of *datum*

1: factual information (as measurements or statistics) used as a basis for reasoning, discussion, or calculation

2: information output by a sensing device or organ that includes both useful and irrelevant or redundant information and must be processed to be meaningful

—Merriam Webster's Collegiate Dictionary

CONNECTING DATA TO SCHOOL IMPROVEMENT

It is irresponsible for a school to mobilize, initiate, and act without any conscious way of determining whether such expenditure of time and energy is having a desirable effect.

—Carl Glickman

As we discussed in the Preface, data have no meaning. The interpretation of data provides information to guide planning and decision making. For educators, organizing and analyzing data is a critical process in any school improvement initiative. However, interpretation is highly subjective and contextual. Data are necessary to calibrate perception. Data, and forums for rich dialogue about the data, illuminate frames of reference and surface individual assumptions, creating space for new ideas and new ways of understanding. Collaborative inquiry into the data supports multiple interpretations of a variety of data sources, increasing understanding and supporting more powerful improvement plans.

There are no truths, only stories.

—Simon Oritz

The collection, examination and interpretation of data informs continual improvement efforts. When collaborative conversations are framed within a spirit of inquiry, educators learn about their students, their practice, their programs and themselves. Prodding, poking and inquiring into what's going on, why its going on and whether it is satisfactory motivates change. A rigorous, data-driven process allows practitioners to better describe the current state of achievement and to identify gaps between the present state and their desired achievement outcomes. And, in the spirit of continuous improvement, there will always be gaps;

between the achievement of individual or groups of students and the high expectations we set for them, between the effectiveness of a particular program or curriculum and the standards identified for successful implementation, between the performance of one school and another, and so on. When colleagues share their observations, consider possible interpretations and explore actions to address moving from where they are to where they want to be, they develop shared understandings of the problem and greater commitment to the developed solutions.

57 Degrees is Data: Hot or Cold is Interpretation

Several years ago, we were working in El Paso, Texas. It was early spring, and phoning home one morning, we found that it was unusually warm for March in New England—57 degrees. Once we arrived at the workshop site, we found the participants filing in wearing hats, gloves and overcoats. As they entered the meeting room, we overheard them greeting each other, exclaiming about the cold weather. It was 57 degrees. 57 degrees is data: hot or cold is interpretation.

DIMENSIONS OF DATA

We are a society that is data rich, but information poor.

—Robert H. Waterman

Schools and school districts are rich in data. A critical part of the data-driven dialogue process is determining how much and what types of data will best serve collaborative inquiry and the group's ultimate outcomes. It is important that the data a group explores are broad enough to offer a rich and deep view of the present state, but not so complex that the process becomes overwhelming and unmanageable. Examining multiple sources that provide several views of the issues under study is important as well. This section describes the multiple dimensions of data and offers some resources, as well as some ways of thinking about the what, why and how of collection.

QUALITATIVE AND QUANTITATIVE DATA

Viewed simplistically, qualitative data relies on description while quantitative data relies on numbers. Not surprisingly, however, it is not quite that simple. Qualitative data tends to be descriptive, holistic and longitudinal. In schools, qualitative data may be found at the school, grade, department, or classroom level. At the school level, items like teacher demographics (years of experience, education, etc.), meeting agendas, memos, schedules and curriculum maps are examples of qualitative data. Grade or department level data might include similar items more specific to the group involved. Classroom and learner-focused qualitative data sources include teacher's anecdotal records, student work samples, portfolios, and so on.

Quantitative data, as the label suggests, is primarily numbers and statistics—things that can be counted and quantified. Quantitative sources include test scores of all types, performance grades, attendance records and enrollment data (see Table 4.1).

Each type of data is organized differently for analysis. Quantitative data uses numbers, percentiles, and other mathematical configurations. These data are organized based on frequency distributions, central tendencies, variabilities and dispersions. For this reason it is easier to create tables, charts and graphs of quantitative data for discussion and analysis purposes. For example, by isolating, or disaggregating, norm-referenced test scores by variables such as gender, race or socioeconomic status, patterns appear within the blur of numbers.

Qualitative data, given its descriptive nature, is usually reviewed holistically, based on the examination of anecdotes and artifacts. For comparative purposes and to discern patterns or trends, one can organize qualitative data by frequency of instances, events, responses, products, etc. Then categories or topics that emerge from the individual items are identified for tables, charts or further investigation. For example, by logging discipline issues by type, time of year, time of day, etc., a clearer picture emerges from the flow of events that is often unseen by those too close to the individual occurrences.

Viewing Data Across Time and Distance

Information Altitudes

Additional dimensions of data include the distance in time or level from the topic under study. Different types of data offer wide-angle or telephoto views of student performance. For example, if we are exploring middle school students' achievement in science, we might look at individual student scores, grade level scores, school-wide scores and perhaps district-wide scores. Each set of scores might include nationally normed indices, such as the California or Iowa Tests of Basic Skills, as well as provincial or state-level scores measuring provincial or state standards, as well as district, school, department or classroom-based tests. Added to this, we might review student work samples, homework assignments, projects, journals and/or portfolios. We think of these measures based on their distance from our initial inquiry and the dimensions of the field of focus. If we investigated the question, "How are our students performing in science at the middle school level?" the individual student work would offer the closest view while the nationally referenced tests, the farthest (see Figure 4.1).

Table 4.1: Examples of Quantitative and Qualitative Data

	EXAMPLES OF QUANTITATIVE DATA	EXAMPLES OF QUALITATIVE DATA
STUDENT PERFORMANCE DATA	A variety of test results including proficiency tests, standardized tests, state exams, district and classroom-based tests The number of students receiving special services, from local, state or federal resources Attendance rates, mobility rates, expulsion rates, suspension rates, drop-out rates Percentage of high school graduates Percentage of students with disabilities who are mainstreamed into regular classes Percentage of retentions or advancements	Student portfolios and other work products Videotapes of student work, performances Exhibitions Student surveys, including pleasure reading inventories, self-esteem stems, self-assessment profiles. Student journals and learning logs Observational records, anecdotals, running records Student interviews Checklists Report card grades
PROGRAM DATA	Teacher-student ratios Numbers of students enrolled in various programs, e.g., advanced placement Head Start, all-day Kindergarten, prevention/intervention programs Teacher/administrator education statistics, e.g., education levels achieved, average number of years with district, average number of years of service overall, number of inductees (first three years), number of retirements expected in the next three years. Teacher participation in professional development activities Budget and resource allocations	Videotapes of special events, classroom, hallways Meeting agendas, minutes, memos Teacher and administrator portfolios Artifacts, e.g., awards, photos of bulletin boards Staff interviews Workshop and training program agendas and evaluations Bulletins and newsletters
COMMUNITY DATA	Data on family demographics, e.g., average income, percentage of single parent families, percentage of two income households Number of school/business and industry partnerships Employment rate; employment sectors in the area	Focus group data Opinion surveys Interviews with parents and community members

THEN AND THERE—HERE AND NOW

Data also have a temporal dimension. That is, we can explore archival data (as described above), we can observe and collect present samples and we can project measurements and tools that will yield information into the future. Once again, if we're interested in exploring the effectiveness of our science instruction, we can look at standardized

Figure 4.1: Information Altitudes

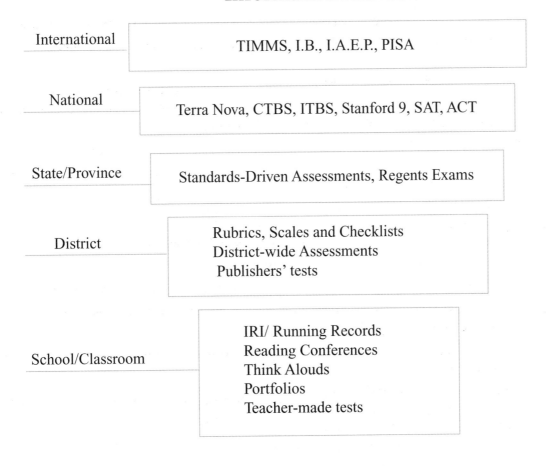

Information Altitudes

International	TIMMS, I.B., I.A.E.P., PISA
National	Terra Nova, CTBS, ITBS, Stanford 9, SAT, ACT
State/Province	Standards-Driven Assessments, Regents Exams
District	Rubrics, Scales and Checklists District-wide Assessments Publishers' tests
School/Classroom	IRI/ Running Records Reading Conferences Think Alouds Portfolios Teacher-made tests

achievement scores for the previous three years to surface trend data (past). We can also conduct surveys regarding students' attitudes towards science and demographic data about the science teachers (present). In addition, we can identify data that will be useful when it becomes available, such as scores on end of grade tests or state science exams (future).

The following section describes archival (or past and readily available) data as well as possibilities for more immediate (or present) data and some collection tools.

ARCHIVAL AND COLLECTIBLE DATA

ARCHIVAL DATA. Archival describes the data that already exist and are accessible as part of the school's established information base, using both quantitative and qualitative sources. Archival data include student performance data and demographic data. Performance data include test results, grades, and even referral, suspension and retention rates.

Demographic data include percentages of students in particular programs, race, ethnicity and gender profiles, attendance rates and socio-economic status (e.g., numbers of students receiving free or reduced lunch). Demographic data for staff might include years of experience and type(s) of certification and level of education. Mobility rates can be accessed for students, staff, and administration.

Archival data also include sources that might offer insight into the workings of the district, school or classrooms. These data have an anthropological quality, and include school correspondence, such as memos, newsletters, bulletins and meeting minutes, descriptions of course offerings and available extracurricular activities. Per pupil expenditures and other budget information fit this category as well.

Archival data have a longitudinal quality and can be accessed and analyzed for trends. For example, a study group might develop a graph comparing student reading scores over five years or a chart indicating the number of students involved in various extracurricular activities for a three year period.

COLLECTIBLE DATA. Collectible data usually sorts out into two categories: behavioral and perceptual. Behavioral data include the workshop sign-in sheets described above. Other examples include frequency of instances of office referral, or percentages of increase, or decrease, in parent attendance at school functions. Checklists and anecdotal records are useful instruments for collecting behavioral data.

Perceptual data include interviews with various groups regarding their feelings, understandings or opinions about a particular issue, innovation or program, such as the student survey of reading confidence described above. Surveys on the degree of satisfaction with the new block schedule, perceptions regarding effectiveness of the present reading program, and parents' responses to interviews on homework policy are additional examples of perceptual data. Interviews and surveys are useful tools for collecting these types of data.

EXPLORING SPECIFIC QUESTIONS

In addition, school archives offer access to data that relate to specific inquiries or improvement efforts. Let's say that a school improvement plan has the goal of increasing mathematics performance. Important data sources might include curriculum maps or lesson plans to determine a baseline on how much time is spent teaching math. This information can be disaggregated, or sub-divided by grade level, percentage of teachers who have been trained in the current math program, or have specializations in that area, and inventories of instructional materials and resources (e.g., which textbooks, kits, and other published materials are being used).

When improvement teams identify an area or areas for exploration, they need to clarify the specific questions that will focus their inquiry. Clear questions point groups towards the most useful data they might collect to shed light on areas of concern. These types of data complement and extend existing data, amplifying understanding. For example, if we want to explore the effect of a district's professional development initiative on students' achievement in reading, we would probably want to access test scores and compare the present year with the previous ones (archival data). We would also want to gather data on the staff participation and training outcomes for specific workshops. We might want to conduct a survey of students' perceived confidence as readers and/or staff members' confidence as teachers of reading. The sign-in sheets and surveys are examples of collectible data.

CHOOSING COLLECTION TOOLS

There are a variety of rich sources offering guidelines, samples and suggestions for choosing and creating collection tools (see References and Resources). While that is not the purpose of this book, we offer the following ideas as a brief list of some possibilities to support further exploration.

INTERVIEWS

The purpose of an interview is to record as fully and fairly as possible each respondent's particular perspective. Interpretation and analysis occur after interview data is organized—never during the interview process. It is important, therefore, to maintain a stance of inquiry when collecting interview data. Interviews vary in their degree of formality (see Table 4.2 and Appendix E: Types of Survey or Interview Questions).

Table 4.2: Three Types of Interviews

INTERVIEW STYLES	RANGING FROM LEAST TO MOST FORMAL
Informal Conversational Interview	Relies on the spontaneous generation of questions in the natural flow of the interaction.
General Guided Interview	Based on an outlined set of issues established in advance which serve as a basic checklist to ensure that the relevant topics are explored.
Standardized Open-ended Interview	Consists of a carefully constructed protocol. The intent is to repeat the same sequence and wording with each interviewee.

SURVEYS

Surveys provide an effective method for collecting both behavioral and perceptual information. Two categories of survey, scaled and unscaled, are most commonly used.

SCALED SURVEY. A scaled survey asks respondents to quantify their answers and provides information that is readily organized graphically. However, these responses are often limited in scope. For example, a response of 4 to the question: "On a scale of 1–5, how would you rate the effectiveness of this program?" does not offer information on what constitutes a 4 for this respondent, or what might have made it a 5.

UNSCALED SURVEY. Unscaled surveys usually require responses to open-ended questions. Compared to scaled surveys, these instruments yield more potential information, but are more complex to organize for analysis. For example, a question might read: "In what ways did this program meet your expectations?" These qualitative data are most often organized into tables or charts based on emerging categories. See Figure 4.2: Qualitative Data Matrix.

Additional collection tools include checklists, anecdotals such as running records and teacher observation logs, videotapes and charts (seating charts, agendas, meeting minutes).

HOW TO CHOOSE DATA

First, determine what you want to know. Once again, this is not quite as simple as it may sound. Sometimes the inquiry process begins with a question, such as: "In what ways does block scheduling affect students' achievement in Social Studies?" or problem statement, such as: "Sixth grade students come to the middle school without the necessary skills for self-directed learning." Or the inquiry process might begin with a hypothesis, such as: "Office referrals would decrease if classroom teachers implemented more cooperatively structured tasks." Each approach still requires the identification of the data needed to explore the issue.

There is also choice regarding the scope of the topic under investigation. For example, a district-level group might want to examine the big picture: "How effective is our social studies curriculum and instruction?" while a school-based team might be most interested in "How has integrating social studies and language arts paid off for third to fifth grade learners?" Herman and Winters (1992) describe these very different approaches as *wide angle* and *close-up*. Wide angle, whether it is at a district, school, department or grade level is often a good beginning for study. Wide angle questions concern the effectiveness of programs for all learners, or large subsets. Examples of wide angle questions include inquiry into achievement gaps among different groups

Figure 4.2: Qualitative Data Matrix

THEME I	THEME II	THEME III	THEME IV

Source Codes:

DATA MATRIX   *Hands-on Science and Student Achievement*   *May 18, 20—*

THEME I: ASSESSMENT	THEME II: TEACHER KNOWLEDGE RE: SCIENCE	THEME III: CURRICULUM	THEME IV: PARENT INVOLVEMENT
	I always loved science in school, so I make sure to do something around science instruction every day. (It-Gr2) *When I teach science, I have to follow the teacher's guide—that way I'm making sure I'm getting it right. (It-Gr4)* *This is my first year teaching—I'm much more conerned about reading and math than I am about science. (It-Gr4)*		*I think its the school's job to teach students. When my kids are home, we do family things. (Sp1)* *I always ask my daughter why she thinks something is happening—or to describe what she sees—you know, about the weather or stuff like that. (Sp.3)*

Source Codes: Interviews: (I); Survey (S), Parent (p), Teachers (t); Student Achievement Tests (CTBS); Science Curriculum Guide (SciCG)

in particular content areas (Are boys outperforming girls in math? Is the rate of enrollment in advanced placement courses for minorities different than that of other groups?) or into major issues for the school population (Is student transiency affecting literacy development? In what ways are temporary teacher certifications affecting student performance, school discipline?)

Once a study group identifies large issues and plans improvement initiatives, exploring close-up questions offers insight into the plan's effectiveness. Often these are the formative questions that lead to refinement and enhancement of an improvement plan. Questions about new methods in assessment (How well do our new performance tasks measure our elementary students' achievement in science?) or instruction (In what ways has the switch to more learner-focused strategies improved performance for special needs students?) are examples in this category.

Most importantly, the inquiries should be clear, and should create conscious curiosity—not fear of reprisal or evaluation. In most instances, just as school improvement efforts connect directly to state standards, so do the collaborative inquiries into data that support them.

RELIABILITY, VALIDITY AND FEASIBILITY

RELIABILITY. Reliability, or the likelihood that the same measures will produce the same results, is a critical factor in choosing data sources. Reliability is one reason that schools tend to rely heavily on norm and criterion referenced tests. These measures are generally reliable across time and for a wide range of students. However, the test items are designed to fit a neutral, objective machine-scoring system, and are limited regarding what they can measure. Open-ended questions or responses requiring inventiveness or creativity do not fit these systems. On the other hand, more authentic measures, such as performance tasks and portfolios, pose a problem when there is little or no inter-rater reliability. This problem occurs if different scorers arrive at different results, or if the same scorer has wide differentiation in findings at different times. Scoring rubrics, exemplars and training sessions designed to increase inter-rater reliability all attempt to address this issue.

VALIDITY. Validity means that the instrument measures what it is designed to measure—that the data reflect what they are intended to show. For example, many fill-in and multiple-choice tests are intended to measure content knowledge, but may be more likely to measure a student's syntactical knowledge or reading ability. Further, although standardized, norm-referenced tests are highly reliable, they may not be valid in measuring sophisticated conceptual understanding or the ability to solve complex problems.

FEASIBILITY. Feasibility is the term for how realistic and reasonable it is to collect and apply a data source. The realities of life in schools create a critical need for making effective and efficient choices. Time, money, energy, and even space come into consideration in making choices about what data to collect. One tip is to look first to archival data, those things that teachers, schools and districts are already collecting and have readily available. After tapping archival resources, groups can make creative and selective choices identifying additional collectibles that will illuminate, detail and complement the existing data.

USING MULTIPLE SOURCES

No individual assessment or measurement instrument is a perfect fit for providing what we want to know about whom and in what ways. Using multiple data sources compensates for the deficits in individual tools and provides a comprehensive picture of the topic under study. Triangulation is a researcher's term for taking at least three different perspectives on an area of study.

TRIANGULATION. One view alone offers a limited, and usually too narrow viewpoint. For example, standardized test scores for School A indicate that 73% of the students in grade four scored proficient or above on the state science exam. A performance ranking of the fourth grade students reveals a clearer understanding of where, within each band, these students performed. Demographic data on each of the students offers even more information about groups that may be marginalized, or specific cohorts whose learning needs are not being met. Triangulation is one way of addressing validity. We can reasonably assume that if three different measures are all indicating similar results, they offer valid information regarding what we want to know.

Triangulating the data is most powerful when the various sources are diverse and varied. Thus, a qualitative measure, such as a student survey, will enhance quantitative measures like state or provincial exams. A third source that is different from either of these, such as teacher anecdotes or a curriculum map, can enhance the view. The idea is to seek multiple sources, using different methods and operating at different levels, or in different areas of the school. Intentionally seeking multiple perspectives, both of the data and those analyzing them, enriches the process and the ultimate outcomes.

EVERYTHING'S RELATIVE: THE ISSUE OF CREDIBILITY

Sensitivity to the many perspectives that group members bring to the table is another important reason for accessing multiple data sources. That is, differences in experience, learning style, educational philosophy, confidence and comfort with using data, as well as diversity in gender, ethnicity, professional position and so on influence a group member's approach to and participation in data-driven inquiry. By combining

Disaggregation is not a problem-solving strategy. It is a problem-finding strategy.
—Victoria Bernhardt

Possible Disaggregates
- *Gender*
- *Grade level*
- *Enrollment in special programs*
- *Ethnicity*
- *School or class*
- *Socioeconomic status*
- *Year of entry into district*

various sources, both qualitative and quantitative, student-centered and system-based, more members of the group can relate to more of the data. In other words, the data are more credible because they are within the scope of individual group member's readiness to accept them.

DISAGGREGATION

Disaggregation is breaking the data apart into smaller subsets. These might be subscores within a larger measure. For example, disaggregated scores are often provided for criterion and norm referenced tests. In addition to the total reading score, we can also look at literal and inferential comprehension or vocabulary skills. Or we might disaggregate based on a specific characteristic, such as viewing math scores by gender or exploring for correlations between reading performance and specific socio-economic groups.

Disaggregation addresses important questions about what is working (or not) and for whom. For example, by disaggregating data by gender, we can determine whether an improvement in math achievement reflects equal gains for males and females. The same questions can be explored for any subset, and helps to determine and ensure that all students have equal access and opportunity to learn.

Disaggregated data give much clearer, more specific information than holistic, lumped together scores. Keep in mind that there are subsets within subsets. It is important to sort a variety of variables, but not so many that the data become overwhelmingly complex, or that the subgroup becomes too small.

VISUALLY VIBRANT INFORMATION

Focusing participants' attention and capturing their energy are two significant challenges to organizing groups around data. In the introduction to his book, The Visual Display of Quantitative Information (1983), Edward Tufte explains, "data graphics visually display measured quantities by means of the combined use of points, lines, a coordinate system, numbers, symbols, words, shading, and color" (p. 9). In our work, we emphasize the importance of creating data graphics as clear visual displays that can be shared by dialogue groups. A ratio of approximately 6–8 participants to one large display of data works to create a focal point. The small group size increases participation and

The idea of display is central. . . . By 'display' we mean spatial formats that present information systematically to the user. Newspapers, gasoline gauges, computer screens and organization charts are all displays. They present information in a compressed, ordered form, so that the user can draw valid conclusions and take needed action.

—Miles & Huberman

captures individual energy. As described in Chapter Two, a large data display serves as a third point, physically separating the group from the data and serving to neutralize it. As a result, the conversation is about what we (colleagues) notice and think about it (the data display). This combination makes it emotionally safer for group members to poke, prod, and question the data and each other.

Table 4.3: Graphic Formats for Visual Data Display

BAR GRAPH 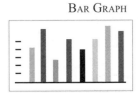	Bar graphs can be used to display comparisons, rankings and change over time. Bars are displayed horizontally or vertically. Stacked bars show the elements that comprise the total. Deviation bar graphs display the data above and below a baseline, or the pluses and minuses of an issue.
LINE GRAPHS 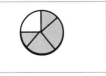	Line graphs display a sloping line, or segments of lines, representing change over time. Thus, they are particularly useful for displaying trends. Line graphs can also display comparisons when several lines are used on the same graph.
PIE CHARTS 	Pie charts display parts of the whole. The size of each part displayed as a percentage makes the relationships among the parts and between the part and whole graphically apparent to observers.
PICTOGRAPHS 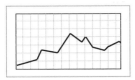	The representation of data as pictures allows for a creative and eye-catching variation from the more commonly used graphs. For example, pictographs can replace the icons on a line graph or can be stacked to form the bars in any form of bar graph.
SCATTER PLOTS 	Scatter plots display relationships between two or more variables. They indicate correlation and comparisons, as one point in time, or over time.
BOX AND WHISKER PLOTS 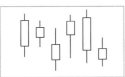	Box and Whisker plots turn raw data into the "shape" of the score distribution for ease of visual interpretation. The boxes display the distribution of scores, while the whiskers indicate the range above and below the median.

Choosing the Visual Representation

Both qualitative and quantitative data can be organized and displayed. Thorough collaborative inquiry usually requires a display that includes both types. Qualitative displays include matrices and relationship charts, such as force-field analysis and consensograms. Quantitative displays include bar, line or pie graphs, dispersion charts and both scatter and box and whisker plots (see Table 4.3). Visual representation is best based on function. The following is a brief description of several commonly used graphing formats. See References and Resources for additional sources of information on this topic.

In most cases, data displays are developed from raw data or, more often, data tables. The display you choose should be closely related to the question, issue or topic being explored. Other visuals include charts and tables, such as frequency charts, disaggregation tables, and curriculum maps. Timelines, schedules, calendars, and other artifacts (e.g., student work samples, meeting minutes, sample memos or newsletters) can also be enlarged to enhance a data display.

Getting Started

Data literacy can be inert—something to know about and talk about— or data literacy can be the knowledge that informs action. Conceptual frameworks without tools and tools without conceptual frameworks each lack value. The three-phase Collaborative Learning Cycle described in Chapter Three provides a conceptual template for guiding rigorous, data-focused, collaborative conversations about school improvement. The skillful application of the tools in the following chapter provide structure for guiding and focusing energy and attention around these important issues.

You don't need an advanced degree in statistics and a roomful of computers to start asking data-based questions about your school, and using what you learn to guide reform.

—Victoria Bernhardt

CHAPTER FIVE—Tools for Teams

"Facilitation is the process of helping a group complete a task, solve a problem or come to agreement to the mutual satisfaction of the participants. Successful facilitation takes preparation and planning, a constructive attitude, certain skills and behaviors, and a collection of process tools."   —Dee Kelsey & Pam Plumb

Skillful facilitators attend to their groups on multiple levels. While creating their plan, they anticipate the emotional, cognitive and energy needs of their participants. Then, during implementation, they monitor the group to determine the effectiveness of their plan. When things are going well, the plan continues. If the meeting is not proceeding as planned, drawing upon a wide repertoire of alternatives supports recovery, increasing capacity for getting back on track, both for the facilitator and the group members.

This chapter is filled with tools, structures, strategies and tips to enhance and extend your facilitative repertoire. The tools in this section are presented alphabetically. Each tool includes logistical information, process directions and guidelines for group work. Many include black line masters for creating overhead transparencies of task directions and for reproducible worksheets. Look for the icon indicating a reproducible resource.

p xx

Information connecting each tool with its contribution to group development is provided, along with variations and applications for specific phases in the Collaborative Learning Cycle. The tools are displayed as a two-page spread. Read the right-hand page for context, logistics and instructions for facilitators. The left-hand page addresses group development. Look for the Collaborative Learning Cycle graphic on each left-hand page to note which phase(s) of the model can be implemented by applying that tool.

Although each tool offers task and process directions, for facilitators there are still a number of choices available and decisions to be made. Some of these decisions relate to the skill level of the group and the skill level of the facilitator. Others are based on the complexity of the task, the available time, the sequence of meetings (first, last, only), and the group's history and experience with the topic and with each other.

There are no recipes for success. However, there are some guidelines that will increase effectiveness and some categories for organizing the planning and implementation decisions. One such category, Managing Decisions, includes three key variables for planning; the size of the group, the length of time and the degree of process structure.

MANAGING DECISIONS

Size of Group

Skillfully navigating between small and full group participation is an important capacity for effective facilitation. Small groupings, such as pairs and trios and even quartets, balance participation, reduce the complexity of interaction and communication patterns and generally allow for a shorter amount of time for task completion. The downside, however, is that there are fewer perspectives and experiences reflected in the group's composition. Larger groups, five or more, require greater participant skill for fluent and productive work, but can benefit from rich and diverse points of view. Planning through a group development lens suggests that novice groups will benefit from frequent experience with paired interactions. Once partners are working effectively, you can create larger groups by combining pairs for Pairs Squared or Pairs Cubed.

Building a repertoire of grouping patterns and grouping strategies, with methods for weaving between task groups and the full group membership, furthers both group development and task production. The suggestions below are intended to support your growing strategy set.

 ### Pairs Squared

Use grouping strategies to create partners. Once pairs are working productively, expand group size into fours or sixes by combining sets of pairs. Capitalizing on the already established partner relationships builds capacity for the complex skills needed to work in larger groups—especially with challenging topics or tasks.

Length of Time

Providing an appropriate length of time for any specific task is always a delicate balancing act. When groups are working independently, it is challenging to coordinate completion time; some groups are finished quickly, while others have hardly begun. Allowing too much time can cause a group to lose focus, while too little can be frustrating. Style preference is a factor in this equation. For some group members and groups there is never enough processing time, while other members value time on task and have little patience with process. As a general rule, a shorter time allotment produces a greater task focus.

Use a Public Timer

Use a public timer to display a countdown while groups are working. This strategy increases focus, supports timely task completion, and makes the groups responsible for managing their time, freeing the facilitator to monitor and interact with working groups.

There are timers made especially for overhead projector display. One source for these timers is: Stokes Publishing Company in Sunnyvale, California (www.Stokespublishing.com).

A low cost software-based timer to use with computer projection is available at Hogbaysoftware.com.

✦ MINUTE FINGERS

When the designated time allotment is up, use the following strategy to poll the group for any need for additional time. Ask group members for a raised hand signal; using a closed fist (we're done); or one to three fingers (we need this many more minutes). The facilitator then averages the time request and adjusts the working time accordingly. Note: Be sure to point out that all members of the task group should be indicating the same time needs.

DEGREE OF STRUCTURE

When groups are clear about your high expectations, they will rise to meet them. Understanding what is expected creates the psychological safety necessary for engaging in challenging work. As you review the strategies in this chapter, as well as those in your present repertoire, consider that for most group processes, the degree of structure can be tightened or loosened. That is, you can increase or decrease the specificity of directions, product requirements, processing protocols, etc. Two criteria regarding this decision are the intended outcome for applying a particular strategy and the level of group skill.

Managing

Decisions

- *Size of Group*
- *Length of Time*
- *Degree of Structure*

INTENDED OUTCOME. When a specific cognitive process or work product is desirable, adjust the strategy's structure and task directions accordingly. Often, task or process directions offer a scaffold for group work, supporting members in achieving more than they might without this structure. For example, if you want groups to summarize, compare and contrast, or invent, build that language into your directions. For these purposes, avoid words like discuss, explore, or consider, which are structurally looser and more open. However, open-ended language is very effective when you want groups to be generative, inventive, and exploratory.

For work products that need to meet specific criteria, explicating the criteria, providing a model or examples and offering a rubric for self-assessment are all strategies that ratchet-up the structure and support group success. Even for a relatively loose structure like brainstorming, providing a number of items to aim for focuses the group energy and increases success with the task.

LEVEL OF GROUP SKILL. Clear, explicit structures support group work. This principle is particularly important when working with novice groups. Protocols that are very specific, especially those that have clear process directions, safeguard individual members. Until trust among group members is established, trust in the process eases emotional tensions and preserves productive task time. For more experienced groups, structured protocols are useful when time is tight, fatigue or stress is high, or the topic at hand may be emotionally charged. One hallmark of expert groups is that they know when it might be useful to apply a tighter protocol and choose one to support the group's work.

PATTERNS OF PARTICIPATION

As described in Chapter Two, skillful facilitators are mindful of the physical, emotional and cognitive energy needs of their groups. Thus, regrouping strategies, and clear, visual task directions are important facilitator tools. Just as the Collaborative Learning Cycle has an Activating and Engaging Phase, so should any design for group work and for the same purposes, to summon and focus emotional and cognitive energy. For example, beginning with a prompt, question, or task that surfaces a participant's individual experiences, ideas, or perspectives is an effective method for bringing that person into the room and establishing readiness. You will note that many of the strategies described in this chapter build this protocol into the task directions. We describe this pattern of individual work, then structured sharing, followed with an opportunity for individual integration of new ideas as a diamond pattern of interaction (see Figure 5.1). Again this organizing and integrating step follows the Collaborative Learning Cycle as well.

For example, a Think, Pair, Share might begin with:

1. Think of one assessment tool you are currently using, besides standardized tests.

2. Meet with a designated partner and share your individual examples. Then, working together, extend your list.

3. Finally, on your own, scan the list and choose one new tool you would be willing to try.

Figure 5.1: A Diamond Pattern of Interaction

Keep in mind that interaction patterns should be varied and purposeful. Too much movement can be distracting, too little, stifling. However, for many participants without a clear purpose or relationship to the work at hand, mixing and moving about feels like a party game. Therefore, especially when readying a group to move, it is always important to clarify your intention, the "What", "Why" and then the "How" as part of your directions.

GROUPING STRATEGIES

There is an endless variety of methods for creating groups. Often, groups are self-selected as people enter the meeting space and choose a seat. Experiment with some of the following strategies when you want to intentionally create or re-create task groups.

PRE-ESTABLISHED GROUPS

Sometimes, it is effective to determine the task groups prior to the meeting. You may want to select and establish groups with a particular composition. For example, a meeting on student assessment could benefit from work groups composed of teachers at different grade levels, forming vertical teams. Or, a district-wide planning team might be divided into task teams with representation from all stakeholders present. For other functions it may be necessary to create groups based on roles in the school, years of experience, content area expertise, etc.

Once you've predetermined a group's composition, you can communicate the decision with group members prior to the meeting with a letter or e-mail. Or, to organize groups on the day of the meeting, post charts with each group's membership in different areas of the room and direct individuals to find their group. Or, for variety, try one of the following ideas:

SYMBOLIC NAME TAGS. Place a number, symbol or colored dot on individual nametags, creating task groups with the same icon. Ask participants to sit with colleagues who have the same designation on their name tag.

THE WEDDING PLAN. As with weddings, or other large social events, place small tags with each participant's name and table number on a welcome table. Place numbered card stock tents on each table. Direct participants to pick-up their tag and find their table.

SELECT SIGN-IN SHEETS. Create a separate sign-in sheet for each task group with a number or some other designator for each sheet. Place the same designators on table tents. When participants sign-in, ask them to join the table group with their symbol.

QUOTE-TABLES. Combine grouping with this Activating and Engaging strategy. Post charts with different quotes related to the meeting topic in different areas of the room. Print different quotes on the cover or somewhere within the participants' materials and ask them to sit in the area matching their quotation. Then, as group members arrive, ask the groups to talk about their interpretation of the quote and ways in which it relates to the topic at hand.

ClipArt is a good resource for theme-based group icons. For example, use a school supplies theme; include group symbols such as a notebook, ruler, calculator, pencil, and blackboard.

DURING THE MEETING

Form groups by organizing participants in a shoulder-to-shoulder line up according to some predetermined criteria (see examples below). Then

- count-off and have like-numbered individuals form a group. For example, counting from 1 through 6 in a group of 24 members will result in groups of four.

  or

- cluster participants in the line to form the group size you require. For example, cluster the first four members in the line to form one group, the second four to form a second group, and so on.

LINE-UPS

Participants line-up in order of a specific variable. Line-ups serve to reorganize work groups as well as build relationship by disclosing some personal information.

Examples include directing participants to line-up in the order of

*O*nce the group is lined-up, count-off, cluster or create a fold to form new tasks teams.

- Their *birthdays* (month and day), from January to December (An interesting twist is to ask participants to complete this line-up without talking)

- Their *street address* (house number), from lowest to highest

- Their *personal preference* for something, from love it to can't stand it (e.g., degree of spice in their food)

- Their *frequency of use* of something, from never to always (e.g., use of writing centers or cooperative learning strategies)

- Their *agreement* with something, from totally disagree to strongly agree (e.g., Students should never wear hats in the classroom)

- The *distance* from where they graduated from high school to the workshop or meeting setting

- Their *estimate* of something, from lowest to highest. Some possibilities include:

  - The number of visitors to a well-known landmark or local tourist attraction

  - Any current factoid that would be relevant to your group and perhaps surprising (e.g., weather statistics, population demographic information, the number of McDonalds in the United States)

Once the group is in line, use a count-off or cluster grouping strategy (as above), or 'fold' the line by bringing the first person face-to-face with the last person in the line and then creating pairs, or clustered groups. The fold is particularly useful for line-ups based on frequency of use, or preference for something, so that the resulting groups are comprised of members with diverse experiences.

MATCHING

Create groups by distributing pre-made materials and directing participants to find the appropriate match(es). Pre-made materials offer variety, interest and relevance to the topic or nature of the group.

MATCHING WITH CARDS

STANDARD DECK. Use a standard deck of cards to establish groups. Distribute the cards and group participants with same numbers, or same suits.

Or create card sets to use and reuse. Consider the following examples for your facilitator's files:

SYMBOL CARDS. Create symbol cards with a variety of colors and shapes. Try a purple square, a red circle, a yellow triangle and a green rectangle. For quartets, have learners locate and join three people with the same shape, or three people with the same color—or they can form a group with four different shapes or colors.

TOPIC CARDS. Create sets that have three or more different pieces of information about one topic. You might create movie cards; one card has a plot synopsis, one has the male and female leads and one has the movie title. Or create animal cards; one card has the habitat, one has a physical description and one has the animal's name. Other possibilities include: city cards; use a famous landmark, geographic location, and city name or literature cards; with genre, author, and book title.

MATCHING WITH WORKSHEETS

Pre-made worksheets offer flexibility and can be tailored for a specific group or topic. Create a worksheet with space for partner sign-ups. Four to twelve symbols can be placed on the page, with a space next to each. Use symbols that are relevant to your group. Use regional, seasonal or topical symbols. For example, for a group of science teachers, create a worksheet with symbols for things you might find in a science lab. Or, in December use holiday motifs (see Reproducible Resource: Meeting Partners).

CHOOSING RECORDERS (AND OTHER ROLES)

To support group work and maximize time it is often efficient to designate a recorder for table teams or other roles as needed, e.g., reporter, supplier, environmental engineer. This process suggestion is indicated in many of the tools for teams that follow. Some possibilities for designating roles include:

NUMBERED HEADS. This cooperative classroom learning strategy (Kagan, 1990) translates well for adult groups. Ask the table members to number-off to their highest number. Use a die, number card or spinner to randomly select a number. The participant with the corresponding number will perform the specified task.

USE CRITERIA. Ask task groups to find the group member who is wearing the brightest color, is the tallest member, has the most fascinating accessories, etc. The designee performs the required task.

Create cards in sets of six. By adding or eliminating cards, you can create pairs, trios, quartets, quintets or sextets.

For assigning roles within the group, choose one particular shape (or color) to be the recorder, another to be the reporter, and so on.

TABLE POSITION. Modeling with one of the table groups, indicate a specific position at the table, for example, the person sitting closest to the exit door, or the middle person on the left side of the table. The indicated individual performs the required task.

SELF-SELECTION. An overriding principle of effective facilitation is to preserve participant choice whenever possible. Toward that end, explain the required task and ask table teams to self-select the member to perform it.

FICKLE FINGER

An effective and light-hearted way to find a reporter, a recorder, or any other designated function for a table group is to use the Fickle Finger. Tell table groups that they are to point to one of their members, on your signal. Explain the role that is needed (e.g., someone to report for your team, someone who had an example that would be useful for all of us to hear) and hold their pointed finger until a count can be made. Individuals with the most fingers pointing at them are the table group's designee.

USE OF SPACE

The physical environment of the meeting space sets expectations from the first moments participants enter the room. A room set up so that group members can face each other and talk easily suggests that face to face conversations are likely to occur. Collaborative work is most effective when there is enough space for separate work groups with room to move about between tables. A good rule of thumb is 30 square feet per participant. Orient the room design so that participants can focus in task groups, and also have good sight lines to a central focal point, such as a screen or podium (see Appendix G: Thinking About Room Design).

Many of the strategies in this chapter call for workstations. Ideally, each workstation would have a table and at least one chart stand. If enough chart stands are not available, look for rooms that have enough wall space for groups to gather around charts taped to the wall.

Create supply bins for each workstation by placing masking tape, highlight pens, markers, sticky-notes of various sizes and any other frequently needed supplies in a plastic bin, or large storage bag for easy distribution and collection. Keep a label on the bin so groups can note replenishment needs. A cost-effective strategy we learned from the staff developers in Kansas City, Kansas is to create mini-rolls of masking tape for each work group by wrapping about $\frac{1}{4}$ of a standard tape roll onto cardboard bobbins. Provide these mini-masking tapes instead of full rolls.

CREATING WORKSTATIONS

A chart stand can be created by turning a rectangular folding table on its short end, balancing the table on one set of legs and folding the top set of legs down.

ENHANCE, EXTEND AND EXPLORE

The array of tools for teams that follows is correlated to the Collaborative Learning Cycle, in terms of the purpose and intention of each. We encourage you to mix and match these strategies with the ones in your existing repertoire, to extend your skill set, to enhance your present practice and to explore new ways of interacting with groups. Look for ways to stack, or sequence strategies to keep participants resourceful and productive (see Appendix C: Strategy Stacks). By definition, a facilitator must be responsive to the group's ever changing tone. The skillful facilitator dances to the tune as someone else is playing it; successful improvisation is supported by sharp attention to the melody and a wide range of potential steps. The strategies following will help keep you on your toes.

Notes

Data-Driven Dialogue: A Facilitator's Guide to Collaborative Inquiry

TOOLS MATRIX	Reproducible	Grouping			Phase of the Cycle			Time			Page #
		Pairs	Small Group	Full Group	Activating and Engaging	Exploring and Discovering	Organizing and Integrating	15-30 minutes	30-45 minutes	45+ minutes	
Annual Review	☐		●			○	○		✓		76
Artifact Hunt	☐		●		○	○				✓	78
Assumption Card Stack and Shuffle	☐		●			○			✓		80
Brainstorm and Pass			●		○			✓			82
Color Question Brainstorm			●		○			✓			84
Consensogram	☐		●		○	○	○			✓	86
Creating Rubrics	☐		●			○			✓		88
First Turn/Last Turn	☐		●			○			✓		90
First Word/Last Word	☐		●		○		○	✓			92
Fishbone	☐		●	●		○			✓		94
Futures Wheel	☐		●			○			✓		96
Here's What/So What/Now What	☐	●			○	○	○		✓		98
Idea, Category, Web	☐		●		○	○	○		✓		100
Interrelationship Diagram	☐		●			○			✓		102
Inter-VENN-tion	☐	●			○	○		✓			104
Matchbook Definitions			●				○	✓			106
Round the Room and Back Again	☐		●	●	○			✓			108
Say Something	☐	●				○		✓			110
Synectics 4-Box	☐		●		○		○	✓			112
Walk-Around Survey	☐		●	●			○		✓		114
Windows and Mirrors			●		○	○		✓			116

ANNUAL REVIEW: UPS AND DOWNS

GROUP DEVELOPMENT

ANNUAL REVIEW gives novice groups a third point to focus upon, as well as a visual summary of multiple perspectives. Scaffolded with discussion questions, novice groups can successfully structure collaborative conversations about their own programs and progress. For skillful groups, the visual provides a focus for an examination of diverse perspectives, assumptions and frames of reference around a particular event, project or period of time.

ATTENTION TO TASK:

The visual display used in this strategy provides an opportunity to gain perspective on highs and lows. The process also establishes a forum and a focus for goal setting.

ATTENTION TO PROCESS:

This strategy fosters reflective practice and balances opportunity for individual reflection with the generation of shared understandings.

ATTENTION TO RELATIONSHIP:

Collaborative review of the group's data display encourages exploration and communicates value for different perspectives on events. The interactive process develops shared understandings of different perspectives—a high point for one person might be a low point for others. Applying this strategy provides a forum where group members can lament the difficulties and celebrate the successes.

MOVING ALONG THE DEVELOPMENTAL CONTINUUM

AS THE GROUP DEVELOPS, YOU MIGHT EXPECT TO SEE/HEAR:

- *critical inquiry about patterns, impact and more proactive future choices*
- *development of insights, expressions of self-awareness and increasing understanding of other's perspectives*

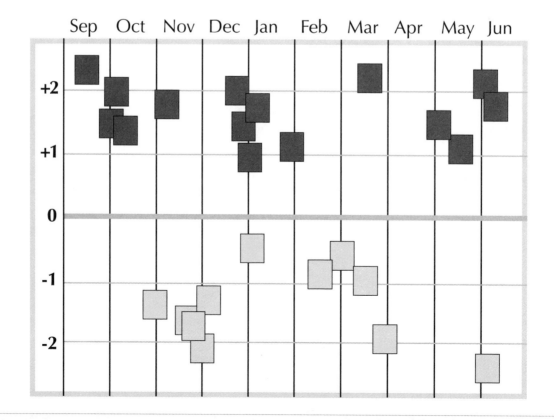

ANNUAL REVIEW: UPS AND DOWNS

A NNUAL REVIEW: Ups and Downs structures an opportunity for shared reflection and assessment of events during a specified period of time. This strategy is appropriate at the midpoint or end of a project, implementation of an initiative or to reflect on the entire school year.

MANAGING:

- *Lay out a grid of five horizontal lines spanning the length of a full wall. (Masking tape or yarn works well for this purpose). Using the center line as the baseline, label the lines above +1 and +2. Label the lines below –1 and –2. Divide the wall chart into time segments, again using masking tape or preprinted labels. For example, if you are reflecting on a traditional school year, the wall would have ten segments, September through June.*
- *Organize table groups of 4–6 participants.*
- *Place sticky notes of two different colors on each table. Each participant will need three notes of each color.*

TIME
30–45 minutes

GROUPING
4–6 participants per task group

MATERIALS
Masking tape or yarn and tacks; sticky notes in two different colors; labels for time segments; open-ended questions on overhead transparency, chart or handout.

pp. 131, 132

INSTRUCTIONS TO FACILITATOR

1. Emphasize to participants that the first step is individual.
2. Direct each group member to think of three high points of the school year. Provide several possible examples. Have them write their high points on one color sticky note—one highlight per note.
3. Repeat this process noting low or challenging points of the school year, written on the second color sticky notes.
4. Once the notes have been posted, structure table group dialogue regarding their observations and impressions of the wall graph.

MODELING:

Provide specific examples of high and low points to ensure that participants understand the kinds of information expected. After group members have completed their individual reflections, model the placement of the notes to create a wall graph of highs and lows.

MONITORING:

Monitor for balanced participation, group engagement, application of appropriate verbal and non-verbal dialogue skills.

MEDIATING:

Display or distribute several open-ended questions designed to deepen and extend the table group conversations. Some examples include:
- *How does the display compare to what you would have expected it to look like?*
- *What are some patterns you're noticing regarding the display?*
- *What are some surprises for you?*
- *How might you compare highs and lows?*
- *What are some generalizations you might make?*

 Facilitator Tip: Create an overhead transparency of the questions or include them in the handout to be used by your group, or do both.

VARIATIONS/APPLICATIONS

- *Modify the process to review a specific project or initiative. Adjust the time segments accordingly (i.e., first six weeks or first marking period).*
- *Use the process to assess the group's development indicating highs and lows of group work during a specific project or period of time.*

ARTIFACT HUNT

GROUP DEVELOPMENT

THE ARTIFACT HUNT provides both novice and more skillful groups with a structure for inquiring into individual and group values. The artifacts provide a safe third point to focus group members' attention and energy. The strategy permits groups to step outside themselves and examine core beliefs and values that can be difficult to discuss.

ATTENTION TO TASK:

The artifact focus makes a highly effective organizer for dialogue and inquiry. The process surfaces many different ideas and perspectives in an efficient manner. It also generates a list of core values and beliefs as a foundation for continued work.

ATTENTION TO PROCESS:

Working in small groups balances participation and increases the individual responsibility of each group member to be both an idea generator and an inquirer into the idea of others.

ATTENTION TO RELATIONSHIP:

Working in small groups makes it safe to share a controversial or divergent idea and makes is safe to inquire into the ideas of others.

MOVING ALONG THE DEVELOPMENTAL CONTINUUM

AS THE GROUP DEVELOPS, YOU MIGHT EXPECT TO SEE/HEAR:

- *group members identify and share possible negative aspects of values deeply held in the work culture*
- *increasing skill with inquiring into the values of others*
- *decreasing storytelling and elaboration*
- *increasing dialogue infused with curiosity and nonjudgmental attitudes*

Notes

ARTIFACT HUNT

A N ARTIFACT HUNT is an anthropological quest to better understand the culture that surrounds an issue, a group, or a plan. This tool offers a reality check for plans and projects by opening a window into the cultural context necessary to implement plans or support intended actions. By examining the symbols and artifacts that hold meaning for participants, group members surface the underlying values that produce and energize key elements of the present culture. The hunt then moves to envisioning the future, seeking ways to amplify the positive aspects of any desired changes. Along the way, there are checks for congruence and incongruence in the system.

TIME
Approximately 45–60 minutes

GROUPING
3–4 participants per task group

MATERIALS
Chart paper and markers (and artifacts provided by participants)

p. 133

MANAGING:

- *Establish groups of 3–4 participants.*
- *Provide chart paper and markers.*

INSTRUCTIONS TO FACILITATOR

1. Describe the essence of anthropological inquiry as it applies to this activity. That is, objects and artifacts hold symbolic meaning that represent underlying values (e.g., a trophy case represents athletic accomplishment, as well as a belief in the importance of heroes, and a value for competition).
2. Direct small groups to collect and or envision artifacts they might show to a visitor from another culture as a means of explaining what is important to their school or organization. These might be examples of events, rituals, routines, or objects that have meaning for their group.
3. Have small groups categorize their collections and label their categories on chart paper.
4. Groups then record the values and beliefs represented by the artifacts within each category. These values might be both positive and negative.
5. Each small group then selects an artifact or artifacts that exemplify important values within the existing state of their culture and share these with the larger group.
6. With reference to the problem, plan or issue under consideration, small groups then identify and select three or four core values within their culture they will need to address in order to successfully implement the plan. These core values may have a positive or negative effect on the plan.
7. When steps 1 through 6 are completed, focus the whole group on a specific date in the future when they might revisit the culture as anthropologists. Have small groups list artifacts, events, rituals and routines they might find as evidence of successful implementation of their plans.

MODELING:

Provide clear examples of artifacts and the values they might represent.
At step four, offer some possible values associated with one category developed by a small group.

MONITORING:

Monitor for balanced participation, group engagement and the use of appropriate verbal and nonverbal inquiry skills. Also monitor and curtail excessive storytelling related to specific artifacts.

MEDIATING:

Small groups will not always agree on the underlying values. Encourage curiosity and nonjudgmental attitudes. Orchestrate full group sharing after the completion of step five and step seven. Apply your own inquiry skills to help both the small and large groups surface the values and beliefs associated with the artifacts.

VARIATION/APPLICATION

Have a working group select and/or generate a starter set of artifacts before the formal meeting. This will jump-start the process and conserve time for the values exploration and the work on envisioning a positive desired state.

ASSUMPTIONS CARD STACK AND SHUFFLE

GROUP DEVELOPMENT

ASSUMPTIONS CARD STACK AND SHUFFLE provides a physical prompt to which group members can react. The dialogue follows individual think time and generation of contributions to the card stack, increasing individual responsibility and balancing participation. For novice groups, process scaffolds increase engagement between group members and ideas.

ATTENTION TO TASK:

This strategy offers group members an opportunity to examine individual and group thinking. It provides a low-risk method for surfacing assumptions, which is a critical element of dialogue.

ATTENTION TO PROCESS:

Assumptions often influence thinking but remain unexamined. Individual completion of the cards makes assumptions explicit. Surfacing and discussing these assumptions often releases individuals and groups from sticking points in any group process. By keeping the assumptions anonymous, the group can explore a viewpoint as separate from an individual.

ATTENTION TO RELATIONSHIP:

By exploring underlying assumptions, group members gain insight into their own and their colleagues' potential limitations regarding any topic or event. Surfacing and inquiring into assumptions broadens understanding of behaviors and viewpoints, leading to more positive interpretations and greater acceptance.

MOVING ALONG THE DEVELOPMENTAL CONTINUUM

AS THE GROUP DEVELOPS, YOU MIGHT EXPECT TO SEE/HEAR:

- *increasing willingness to share personal assumptions*
- *increasing skillfulness in inquiring into other's assumptions*
- *increasing sensitivity to different ways of thinking about the topic*
- *expression of insights about the constraints and limitations of the topic at hand*

Notes

ASSUMPTIONS CARD STACK AND SHUFFLE

ASSUMPTIONS CARD STACK AND SHUFFLE provides a structured process for surfacing the assumptions and beliefs that underlie and often constrain thinking. Individuals and groups get an opportunity to articulate, explore, and question their assumptions.

MANAGING:

• *Organize table groups of 4–6 participants.*
• *Place a stack of index cards on each table, providing at least 2–3 for each group member.*

TIME
30–45 minutes

GROUPING
4–6 participants per task group

MATERIALS
Index cards; sentence strips (see variations)

pp. 134, 135

INSTRUCTIONS TO FACILITATOR

1. Direct participants to distribute blank index cards evenly among the table group members.
2. Individually, participants create a stack of cards that hold some of their assumptions about the topic under discussion. Emphasize that there should be only one assumption per card.
3. Have group members pool their cards in the center of the table.
4. After shuffling the collective deck, place all cards in the center of the table.
5. In turn, each group member picks a card to read aloud to the table group. Members engage in dialogue and/or discussion about the items.

MODELING:

Make your own assumptions explicit as you speak with the group. Label assumptions of others as part of your response, with phrases like, "so one assumption you're making is that . . ." or "given your description, you seem to be assuming that . . ."

MONITORING:

Observe to be sure that participation is balanced. Encourage groups to draw another card if momentum seems to be waning. Monitor for group engagement and application of appropriate verbal and non-verbal dialogue skills. Inquire into assumptions as participants share opinions and perspectives. Be sure to use an invitational stance and be sensitive to the need for emotional safety.

MEDIATING:

Display or distribute several open-ended questions designed to deepen and extend the table group conversations. Some examples include:
• *What is the thinking behind this assumption?*
• *What are some inferences that can be made from it?*
• *What might be some alternative interpretations?*
• *To what degree is this assumption generalizable or context specific?*
• *If _____ were true, would this assumption still hold?*

VARIATIONS/APPLICATIONS

• *Collect all the cards and distribute them randomly, so table groups are working with assumptions they did not necessarily generate.*
• *Create an Assumptions Wall. After 25–30 minutes, have group choose one or two assumptions to transfer to sentence strips for display. Structure a full group dialogue around these assumptions. See mediative questions above.*
• *Replace assumptions with other information. For example, use the Card Stack and Shuffle process to Activate and Engage thinking by replacing assumptions with predictions prior to viewing data. Or, use the Card Stack and Shuffle process to Organize and Integrate thinking by replacing assumptions with reflections regarding the initiative, or significant learning regarding experiences with the topic.*

BRAINSTORM AND PASS

Organizing and Integrating

Activating and Engaging

Exploring and Discovering

GROUP DEVELOPMENT

BRAINSTORM AND PASS is an effective way to increase participation and prevent individuals who are most vocal, most knowledgeable or most passionate about a topic from dominating the session.

ATTENTION TO TASK:

In addition to focusing a group on the topic and generating information for later use, this strategy produces creative and unusual ideas.

ATTENTION TO PROCESS:

This strategy scaffolds group members' capacity to slow down and listen to each other. It provides think time for individuals who may be less verbal, or who process internally before speaking.

ATTENTION TO RELATIONSHIP:

This strategy highlights the value of nonjudgmental interactions and emphasizes the power of collective idea generation.

MOVING ALONG THE DEVELOPMENTAL CONTINUUM

AS THE GROUP DEVELOPS, YOU MIGHT EXPECT TO SEE/HEAR:

* *increasing comfort with longer pauses*
* *greater appreciation for diverse thinking*
* *increased merging with and extending on other's ideas*

Notes

BRAINSTORM AND PASS

B RAINSTORM AND PASS capitalizes on the creative, generative qualities of the brainstorming process while creating a structure for inclusion of all participants. Use Brainstorm and Pass any time you might use the traditional brainstorming process. This strategy effectively increases participation and prevents individuals who are most knowledgeable, passionate or vocal about a topic to dominate the thinking.

MANAGING:

Establish table groups of 6–8 participants.

TIME
5 minutes

GROUPING
6–8 participants per task group

MATERIALS
note paper

INSTRUCTIONS TO FACILITATOR

1. Review ground rules for brainstorming.
2. Choose a recorder, using whatever strategy you prefer.
3. Describe the round-robin process using an overhead transparency as a visual aid. Explain that group members will offer ideas on the topic in turn, starting to the right of the recorder. The group must wait for each member to either a) contribute an idea or b) say "Pass". Emphasize that passing is just for the moment, and individuals who pass still get a turn on the next go around. Note: The recorder is also included in the brainstorm process.
4. After approximately 3 minutes, call "time's up."

 Facilitator Tips: Set a minimum target for number of ideas to be generated. Keep time short to maximize attention and focus.

MODELING:

Explicitly mark a round-robin pattern for sharing by beginning to the right of the recorder.

MONITORING:

Observe the group for attention to process—taking turns, honoring wait time and no blurting or cross talk. Monitor for judging, explaining, defending or elaborating of ideas.

MEDIATING:

Remind participants to allow brief think time and honor the choice to pass, rather than "saving" a colleague by offering their own idea. It is important to emphasize the nonjudgmental quality of brainstorming and acceptance of all ideas at this stage.

VARIATIONS/APPLICATIONS

* Rather than having one recorder, pass the pen and paper around the table.
* Create charting stations for a public list. Use chart stands or charts taped to the wall.
* After the small group process, add a full group dimension by having table groups share items from their lists, in turn, until all ideas have been charted.
* Brainstorm and Categorize. Add another dimension by shifting the thinking process from generating ideas to categorizing those that have been generated. Use the categories for discussion purposes, for further exploration, or with another tool, such as Fishbone Diagram.

COLOR QUESTION BRAINSTORMING

Organizing and Integrating

Activating and Engaging

Exploring and Discovering

GROUP DEVELOPMENT

COLOR QUESTION BRAINSTORMING reinforces the continual learning produced by generating questions, rather than answers, particularly for novice groups. The brainstorming pattern keeps it open-ended and non-judgmental. When these protocols are followed, divergent perspectives and unexamined assumptions are often revealed.

For more experienced groups, the process pushes past potential stuck points. Because groups tend to favor particular types or categories of thinking, this strategy supports a vision beyond any unintended blind spots.

ATTENTION TO TASK:

Color Question Brainstorming increases a group's consciousness about the complexity of issues and the complexities of thought required to deal with them. Ultimately, a richer exploration of a problem, as well as a more effective solution results.

ATTENTION TO PROCESS:

Brainstorming, by definition, engages a group in divergent thinking. It is a psychologically safe process for surfacing unexamined ideas and encouraging creative possibilities. The brainstorming protocol reinforces a nonjudgmental approach during the initial stages of problem solving.

ATTENTION TO RELATIONSHIP:

This process illuminates the importance of different thinking and learning styles to productive group work. Group members grow to appreciate those colleagues who think differently than they do.

MOVING ALONG THE DEVELOPMENTAL CONTINUUM

AS THE GROUP DEVELOPS, YOU MIGHT EXPECT TO SEE/HEAR:

- *frequent pausing to allow the less vocal members to add ideas*
- *increasing piggybacking on other's ideas to produce a wider range of questions in each category*

Notes

COLOR QUESTION BRAINSTORMING

COLOR QUESTION BRAINSTORMING uses a traditional brainstorming process. However, rather than generating ideas or answers, the group focuses its generative energies to develop questions. Based on the work of Jerry Rhodes, this strategy directs the question brainstorming into three distinct categories, each related to a different color. These 'colors of the mind' produce a wide range of questions and push the boundaries for any group.

MANAGING:

- *Organize task stations with three sheets of chart paper, labeled with each question category.*
    - *Green Questions: Imagination, Ingenuity, Possibility*
    - *Red Questions: Facts, Figures, Data*
    - *Blue Questions: Judgments, Opinions, Values, Needs*
- *Create task groups of 6–8 participants.*

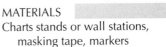

TIME
15–30 minutes

GROUPING
6–8 participants per task group

MATERIALS
Charts stands or wall stations, masking tape, markers

INSTRUCTIONS TO FACILITATOR

1. Explain the question categories, and remind the group of the brainstorming process.
2. Direct groups to brainstorm a large quantity of questions (remember, no judgment), beginning with whatever chart/category they prefer, and working with one chart/category at a time.

Facilitator's Tip: It is often effective to abbreviate and synchronize the brainstorming period. For example, after groups brainstorm on one chart for four minutes, call time and direct them to the next chart, and so on.

3. After the designated time, groups step back and examine their lists, highlighting or circling the questions that seem most relevant to the issue at hand.
4. Additional questions may be added at this time.

MODELING:

Provide stems for, or examples of, each type of question. Some examples include:

Green	What might happen if we . . .	*"What might happen if we changed the school schedule to create longer days in a four day week?"*
Red	How many . . . How much . . .;	*"How many students took advanced placement tests during the last school year?"* *"What percentage of our high school graduates go on to four year colleges?"*
Blue	Why is this . . . What's the best way to . . . ?	*"Why is this the way we sequence math for the ninth grade?"* *"What's the best way to organize student portfolios?"*

MONITORING:

Monitor for application of brainstorming protocols, ensuring that group members are not describing, defending or explaining their items. Pay attention to be sure that participation is balanced, and that the bulk of questions does not come from just a few individuals. For some groups, it is useful to scaffold the brainstorming with a physical prompt (e.g., pass around a koosh ball and add an idea when you receive it) or a structure like Brainstorm and Pass (see pages 82–83).

MEDIATING:

As you walk around to each task group, inquire for deeper or more divergent thinking. Push groups to develop questions in new and unexpected directions. Particularly in the green and blue categories, "what if" questions can nudge the thinking into unimagined areas.

VARIATIONS/APPLICATIONS

- *Insert a Walk-About between steps 3 and 4 so that groups can learn from each other's thinking.*
- *Question Brainstorming: This strategy follows the same process, without the organizational schema of the colors. Task groups brainstorm as many questions as they can about the topic under consideration. Then, the group categorizes the questions according to its own schema.*

CONSENSOGRAM

Organizing and Integrating

Activating and Engaging

Exploring and Discovering

GROUP DEVELOPMENT

THE CONSENSOGRAM strategy develops a climate of conscious curiosity and purposeful uncertainty within the group. The graphs establish shared points of reference, focusing energy and attention on ideas and perceptions not on each other. Consensograms produce a visually vibrant focal point for group dialogue.

ATTENTION TO TASK:

Generating the Consensogram questions clarifies critical dimensions of an issue, problem, or change initiative for facilitators and group leaders. The graphic displays facilitate exploration of the tensions within individuals and the group related to issues, problems, and change initiatives.

ATTENTION TO PROCESS:

This model of inquiry encourages observation and analysis skills such as comparing and contrasting. Productive inquiry requires that individuals and groups suspend their need to assign causality or have immediate closure on issues. This process increases group members' capacities for open-ended inquiry and compassionate curiosity about the ideas and positions of others.

ATTENTION TO RELATIONSHIP:

This strategy surfaces a wide range of possible stances regarding an issue, promoting a sense of inclusiveness within the group. The positioning of the sticky notes or adhesive color dots alerts both individuals and the group to the presence of minority perspectives. This awareness includes the outliers themselves. The inquiry phase normalizes introspection, honesty, and appreciation of diverse opinions.

MOVING ALONG THE DEVELOPMENTAL CONTINUUM

AS THE GROUP DEVELOPS, YOU MIGHT EXPECT TO SEE/HEAR:

- *increasing willingness by individuals to be open and honest in their responses to the Consensogram questions; this includes an increasing comfort with taking outlier positions*
- *increasing willingness and skill in pursuing a stance of conscious curiosity, especially for opinions or positions that vary from expectations or any group norm*
- *increasing use of paraphrasing of previous comments prior to adding thoughts or inquiring*
- *greater comfort with extended pauses between comments*

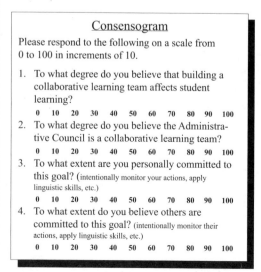

Consensogram

Please respond to the following on a scale from 0 to 100 in increments of 10.

1. To what degree do you believe that building a collaborative learning team affects student learning?
   0 10 20 30 40 50 60 70 80 90 100
2. To what degree do you believe the Administrative Council is a collaborative learning team?
   0 10 20 30 40 50 60 70 80 90 100
3. To what extent are you personally committed to this goal? (intentionally monitor your actions, apply linguistic skills, etc.)
   0 10 20 30 40 50 60 70 80 90 100
4. To what extent do you believe others are committed to this goal? (intentionally monitor their actions, apply linguistic skills, etc.)
   0 10 20 30 40 50 60 70 80 90 100

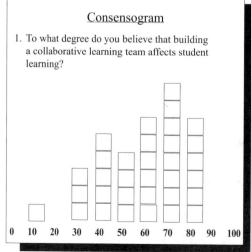

Consensogram

1. To what degree do you believe that building a collaborative learning team affects student learning?

0 10 20 30 40 50 60 70 80 90 100

Facilitator Tip: Effective consensogram questions surface the tensions within the group regarding specific questions and between questions. For this reason, juxtaposing perspectives such as self versus others, immediate versus long term and interest versus knowledge create powerful dynamics for productive dialogue.

CONSENSOGRAM

CONSENSOGRAMS vividly display data generated by a group as bar graphs, creating a focal point for dialogue. The data represent group members' perceptions of commitment, belief, interest or skill level related to an issue, problem or change initiative. Consensogram questions can originate from a variety of sources including the facilitator, organizational leaders, or group members. The consensogram starts, structures and sustains thinking in the conversation.

MANAGING:

- *Craft three to five consensogram questions to which participants can respond on a 0–100 scale. The most effective questions surface levels of skill, interest, knowledge, commitment, belief, importance, or values.*
- *Reproduce a worksheet for each participant with consensogram questions and scales.*
- *Prepare large charts for displaying group data as bar graphs. Place each question as a heading and a 0–100 scale on the bottom.*
- *Organize table groups of 6–8 participants representing a variety of roles and perspectives.*
- *Have ready enough sticky notes or adhesive color dots for individual transfer of responses to the appropriate column on the group graphs.*

TIME:
Approximately 45 minutes

GROUPING:
6–8 participants per task group

MATERIALS:
- Transparency of task directions. Note: It is also useful to have an overhead transparency of the worksheet.
- One worksheet per participant
- Sticky notes or adhesive color dots (one per question times the number of participants)
- A chart for each question displayed on the wall or clustered chart stands

p. 136

INSTRUCTIONS TO THE FACILITATOR

1. Provide each member of the group with a sticky note or adhesive dot for each question to be explored. (Be sure the sticky notes or dots are all the same size).
2. Display the questions for consideration on a chart or overhead.
3. Direct participants to individually respond to each question, based on their own perceptions, using the scale of 0–100. Responses must be in increments of 10, with no negative numbers.
4. Have participants place their 0–100 responses on a sticky note or color dot corresponding to each specific question.
5. Participants then place their sticky note or dots on the prepared charts in the appropriate columns, forming bar graphs.
6. When all responses have been posted and the graphs are complete, organize a group exploration of the data. See the mediating section below for sample questions to guide this phase.

 Facilitator's Tip: Providing an Activating and Engaging phase is critical to success. This is true whether or not the task design applies the full Collaborative Learning Cycle. Many of the strategies in this book serve this function, or use the Activating and Engaging questions from the Model (p. 44).

MODELING:

It is useful to demonstrate precise positioning of the sticky note or dots to ensure proper alignment of the bar graphs.

MONITORING:

As groups explore the data, pay attention to the balance of participation within the task groups. Listen for intonation that indicates curiosity, rather than certainty, as group members share observations, suggest inferences, and propose cause/ effect relationships.

MEDIATING:

The intention of this strategy is to structure exploration and discovery of group member's perceptions about an issue, problem or change initiative. The following questions guide group interaction:
- *What are some of your predictions and assumptions?*
- *What are some of the things you are noticing about the data on the graphs?*
- *What important points seem to pop-out?*
- *What are some patterns, categories or trends that are emerging?*
- *What seems to be surprising or unexpected?*
- *What are some things we have not yet explored?*

CREATING RUBRICS

Organizing and Integrating

Activating and Engaging

Exploring and Discovering

GROUP DEVELOPMENT

CREATING RUBRICS provides a forum for conversations about high standards. For novice groups, completing the graphic format maximizes task focus. For more skillful groups, clearly defining a high and low end stretches boundaries and pushes exploration of preconceived notions.

ATTENTION TO TASK:

Implementation of this strategy produces an assessment tool. The discussion that produces the tool defines abstractions and creates practical indicators for continued group work.

ATTENTION TO PROCESS:

Creating a rubric provides a common language to help diverse groups talk about a complex process or concept. The Rubric is a tangible reflection of the group's attention to process.

ATTENTION TO RELATIONSHIP:

Creating Rubrics gives rise to discourse about the individual and collective values and beliefs that define practice and determine behaviors. The protocol provides an emotionally safe method for surfacing and exploring these deeply held values and beliefs, increasing flexibility and opening the possibility for new ideas and understandings.

MOVING ALONG THE DEVELOPMENTAL CONTINUUM

AS THE GROUP DEVELOPS, YOU MIGHT EXPECT TO SEE/HEAR:

- *increasing comfort with sharing personal criteria*
- *increasing willingness to collaborate on refining criteria*
- *increasing skill and comfort with probing for specificity*
- *decreasing storytelling and elaboration of examples*

Developing Dialogue Capacities

	Burlap	Corduroy	Velvet
Primary Trait Communication is balanced and directed toward shared understanding.			

CREATING RUBRICS

THE NAME RUBRIC derives from the fourteenth century Middle English rubrick, the red ocher used at that time for tinting headings in books, most often for liturgical services. These red markings indicated the proper cadence for reading a passage or singing a hymn. The word has evolved to indicate an established rule, tradition or custom. In educational lexicon, a rubric provides a way to define excellence, especially in dealing with processes or abstract concepts. Creating Rubrics provides a focus for group exploration of standards and criteria for success. Use Creating Rubrics as a process for developing a formative or summative tool for group reflection.

TIME
30–45 Minutes

GROUPING
4–8 participants per task group

MATERIALS
chart paper, markers, masking tape and/or chart stands for stations

p. 137

MANAGING:

- *Prepare chart paper, markers and masking tape for each table group.*
- *Use an overhead transparency to display the rubric format to describe the task.*

INSTRUCTIONS TO FACILITATOR

1. Describe the purposes of a rubric, and share an example or two. Keep in mind many educators are familiar with rubrics for classroom use. Check group members' experience, and suggest they draw from it.
2. Identify the critical attributes or categories for which scales will be developed.
3. Provide, or have the group suggest, a scale. A range of numbers (e.g., one to four) or labels (e.g., not yet/competent/excellent) works well.

 Facilitator's Tip: Be playful with labels. For example, you can use burlap (still rough), corduroy (a bit bumpy) and velvet (really smooth) as your scale. This approach helps keep group members psychologically safe.

4. Direct the task groups to generate qualities for the top end of the scale first, then the bottom, then fill-in. In this way, if time is short, the most important conversation (what constitutes excellence) has been discussed.
5. After a designated amount of time, facilitate a full group exploration of each rubric. You might use a walk-about or mini-presentation by each group.
6. Finally, groups can refine their own rubrics, or you can work towards consensus on one for the full group.

MODELING:

Have ready samples of rubrics.

MEDIATING:

Scaffold group work by providing rubric language (see appendix).

VARIATIONS/APPLICATIONS

- *Create rubrics for dialogue prior to engaging collaborative inquiry. In this way, groups can use their own rubrics for self-assessment and reflection on their process.*
- *Other applications include creating rubrics for any abstract concept, (e.g., academic excellence, positive community relationships, classroom management).*

FIRST TURN/LAST TURN

Organizing and Integrating

Activating and Engaging

Exploring and Discovering

GROUP DEVELOPMENT

THE FIRST TURN/LAST TURN strategy supports novice groups in developing norms of dialogue and experiencing the essence of collaborative inquiry. It is also useful for more experienced groups when they are dealing with emotionally charged or technically complex information. The restriction of cross talk honors the contribution of each group member to the whole that is emerging.

ATTENTION TO TASK:

This strategy supports groups by presenting and investigating information in a non-threatening manner. The structure minimizes off-task comments and nonessential elaboration.

ATTENTION TO PROCESS:

Collaborative inquiry requires attentive listening and respect for the ideas of others. This strategy structures an environment for listening and being listened to. The round-robin pattern slows the pace of response, providing individuals with time for reflection and a protected space within which to offer comments.

ATTENTION TO RELATIONSHIP:

Listening to others without commenting is not a well-established habit in most groups. Within the First Turn/Last Turn process, some group members, especially those with high relationship needs or passionate opinions about the content, will be challenged by the constraints of this process. Anticipate this tension and proactively acknowledge and highlight it during the task directions and process modeling demonstration.

MOVING ALONG THE DEVELOPMENTAL CONTINUUM

AS THE GROUP DEVELOPS, YOU MIGHT EXPECT TO SEE/HEAR:

- *increasing comfort with silence and longer pauses between speakers*
- *increasingly substantive responses to the content and to previous comments*
- *paraphrasing of previous comments prior to adding thoughts*
- *comments about the comments as individuals become more comfortable being metacognitive about emerging ideas and patterns of thought*
- *increasing comfort by group members in sharing controversial observations or opinions*

Notes

FIRST TURN/LAST TURN

FIRST TURN/LAST TURN is a structured process for engaging in dialogue and collaborative inquiry. It develops an appreciation for the power of listening and the personal and shared learning possibilities in exploring diverse perspectives. This strategy provides a clear protocol that is especially helpful for newly forming groups and for any groups working with controversial topics or technically complex information.

MANAGING:

- *Select relevant information (e.g. text, data sets, student work samples).*
- *Organize table groups of 6–8 participants representing a variety of roles and perspectives.*
- *Distribute materials to participants.*

TIME
Approximately 30–45 minutes

GROUPING
6–8 participants per task group

MATERIALS
Transparency of task directions
A copy of selected materials for
    each group member
Highlight pens   *p. 138*

INSTRUCTIONS TO FACILITATOR

1. Have task group members individually read/examine the selected material, highlighting 2–3 items. Items could be points of agreement, points of disagreement, provocative statements, interesting facts, or curiosities.
2. Describe and model the round-robin process. Emphasize the restriction of cross talk.
3. Determine the first speaker. Some options include: numbering-off and randomly selecting a starting number, group designates, participant volunteers or facilitator's choice.

 Facilitator Tip: It is often useful to designate the starting speaker. These individuals set the tone (integrity of process, quality of response) for the remainder of the group. Their positive modeling increases the likelihood of honoring the process.

Consider who will go first (naming a point of interest) and who will go second, (commenting on the designated passage). It is generally not desirable to establish a response pattern in which an individual with role authority is the initial or second speaker. In many cases this pattern inhibits the responses of other group members.

4. Run the process for a designated time period. The complexity of text materials, experience of group members, familiarity with the structure and/or topic and length of time of the meeting are all variables in determining time allotment. Be sure to inform the group that not everyone will necessarily have a chance to initiate a comment.
5. Reconvene the full group for process/content reflections.

MODELING:

Physically demonstrate the round-robin process with one task group, standing behind each group member to simulate the pattern of participation. Clearly designate the starting person for the groups.

MONITORING:

Scan groups for consistent application of the round-robin process. Look for one person speaking at a time with no cross-conversations.

MEDIATING:

Intervene with groups if you hear cross talk or conversation that violates the round-robin pattern. If a task group is not correctly implementing the process, gently share your observation of its behavior. Inquire about where members are in the process, or what might be causing tension or difficulty.

VARIATIONS/APPLICATIONS

- *You can use the First Turn/Last Turn to explore a variety of information sources, including:*
    - *research selections or syntheses*
    - *articles from journals or newspapers*
    - *student work samples*
    - *data sets (graphs, tables, aggregated survey results, etc)*
- *As an option to verbally sharing ideas about the content, groups can use the Matchbook Definitions tool to capture their thinking.*

FIRST WORD/LAST WORD

Organizing and Integrating

Activating and Engaging

Exploring and Discovering

GROUP DEVELOPMENT

FIRST WORD/LAST WORD surfaces and/or organizes important concepts, principles, and understandings about a topic. Posting the charts supports group memory. This approach enriches the group's knowledge base, establishing a collective reference system.

ATTENTION TO TASK:

This strategy develops common language, promotes shared definitions, and delineates specific attributes for the topic at hand. It reinforces and increases shared knowledge about a topic or concept.

ATTENTION TO PROCESS:

The First Word/Last Word protocol supports a group in analyzing and defining abstract topics. The push for elaboration surfaces insights and enhances clarity of understanding for individuals and the group.

ATTENTION TO RELATIONSHIP:

This strategy requires both idea people and language people, honoring the need for diverse abilities in group work. Expanding from small group production to large group sharing capitalizes on the productivity of task groups, while maintaining a common focus and identity as a community.

MOVING ALONG THE DEVELOPMENTAL CONTINUUM

AS THE GROUP DEVELOPS, YOU MIGHT EXPECT TO SEE/HEAR:

- *increasing editing, revising and refining of ideas*
- *intentional alternation between generating details and exploring conceptual fit*
- *purposeful searching for what might be missing*
- *shifting from task completion to deeper understanding as the goal*

> **D** oesn't require agreement
>
> **I** nquiry sparks sharing
>
> **A** ttending inside and outside ourselves is key
>
> **L** istening to others' ideas is important
>
> **O** penness to alternative perspectives is encouraged
>
> **G** oes to unexpected places
>
> **U** nderstanding emerges through the process
>
> **E** ngages intellect and emotion

FIRST WORD/LAST WORD

IRST WORD/LAST WORD is an adaptation of traditional acrostics. Task groups generate phrases that begin with each letter in the designated word, elaborating important dimensions of the topic or concept being explored. This process can be applied as an Activating and Engaging strategy to start the conversation or as an Organizing and Integrating strategy to synthesize thinking in a meeting or work session.

MANAGING:

- *Write the topic word vertically down the left hand side of a large chart paper or overhead transparency.*
- *Organize table groups of 4–6 participants.*

TIME
Approximately 20–25 minutes

GROUPING
4–6 participants per task group

MATERIALS:
A recording sheet for each task group (optional).

INSTRUCTIONS TO FACILITATOR

1. Determine a recorder (Some options include: numbering-off and using random selection, group designee, participant volunteer or facilitator's choice).
2. Have recorders create a work sheet for their table group, duplicating the model on the chart or overhead projector.
3. Task groups generate phrases that begin with each letter in the designated word, elaborating important dimensions of the topic or concept being explored.
4. After 8–12 minutes, refocus the group for sharing.

MODELING:

Model a sample phrase for one or two of the letters to set a standard for both quality and quantity of response.

MONITORING:

Because this strategy is so closely related to acrostics, it is important to be sure that groups craft extended phrases or sentences that relate to the topic, not just single words, beginning with each letter.

MEDIATING:

Encourage the group to generate important attributes, characteristics or ideas related to the topic prior to organizing these associations into phrases. This concept word bank becomes the source material for crafting phrases. This option is especially useful when using this strategy as the Last Word.

VARIATIONS/APPLICATIONS

- *If time is limited, assign a different section of the word to each group; or have half the room begin from the top down, and the other half from the bottom up.*
- *Have groups complete their work on large charts and post for sharing and/or reference.*

FISHBONE/CAUSE-EFFECT DIAGRAMS

GROUP DEVELOPMENT

FOR BOTH NOVICE and expert groups, the Fishbone Diagram provides a third point to focus group work. It visually displays the complex dynamics of interrelated elements in a system, increasing the capacity of the group members to view a problem with a systems lens. Most importantly, it focuses the group on the causes—not the symptoms.

ATTENTION TO TASK:

Understanding the causal structure of a presenting problem is a necessary prerequisite to addressing it. This strategy offers a time-effective process for exploring multiple dimensions of a problem or issue, revealing important relationships among various variable and potential causes.

ATTENTION TO PROCESS:

The brainstorming stages of this process foster flexible thinking, freeing groups from preconceived solutions. The comprehensive lens of seeking multiple causes, both broad and specific, result in deeper understandings of the problem, as well as a more satisfying pursuit of solutions.

ATTENTION TO RELATIONSHIP:

The Fishbone organizes and displays various theories of causality, allowing group members to step back from their personal preferences and consider a variety of possibilities. This visual representation reduces the personal focus and provides the third point for all team members to nonjudgmentally review relationships and root causes before moving to solution seeking.

MOVING ALONG THE DEVELOPMENTAL CONTINUUM

AS THE GROUP DEVELOPS, YOU MIGHT EXPECT TO SEE AND HEAR:

- *multiple and unusual causal roots developed and explored*
- *decreasing use of personal storytelling and explanations*
- *group members seeking and expressing value for diverse possibilities*

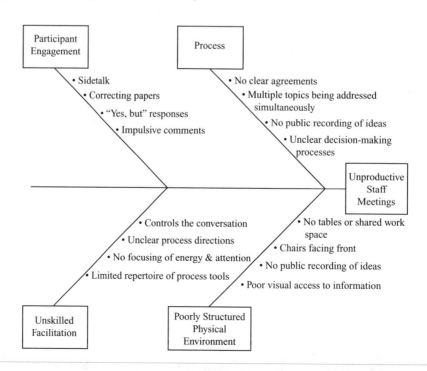

FISHBONE/CAUSE-EFFECT DIAGRAMS

THE FISHBONE or Cause-Effect Diagram was originally conceived by Kaoru Ishikawa, an early pioneer of quality management processes in the Kawasaki shipyards. The diagram visually represents the relationships between a particular effect and its potential causes. Use the Fishbone diagram when a group needs to identify and explore the possible causes of a problem or existing condition. The graphic display provides a third point for group focus.

MANAGING:

- *Establish groups of 4–6 participants. Note: Depending on group size, you can create one Fishbone Diagram with the entire group.*
- *Set-up stations with chart stands or charts on the wall.*

INSTRUCTIONS TO FACILITATOR

1. Identify a condition or problem for which the group will be generating possible causes. Note: The group may have previously identified this topic.
2. Generate the possible causes using a brainstorming process.
3. Categorize the causes into 4–6 major categories. Note: you may want to provide the categories, and then have groups place their brainstormed ideas on the category 'fishbone'.
4. Construct the Fishbone Diagram (or direct each task group to construct its own) as follows:
   a. Place the problem statement in a box on the right side of the chart (the head of the fish). Draw a straight line, or spine, from the head to the tail.
   b. Draw one fishbone for each cause category angled away from the spine. Place the major causal category labels in a box at the end of each fishbone.
   c. Fill in the specific causes related to each category along each fishbone. Note: it is possible that a specific cause will be placed in more than one category.
5. Review each major cause category. Circle the most likely causes and explore the reasons that they are a cause.

TIME:
30–45 minutes

GROUPING:
Full group; or task groups of 4–6

MATERIALS:
Chart paper or overhead transparency of fishbone; markers, masking tape

p. 139

MODELING:

- *Develop a Fishbone Diagram with the full group, using a topic that is not necessarily related to the topic under study. Consider topics about which the group will be knowledgeable and with which the group will be comfortable, for example, a successful dinner party.*
- *Prepare a chart or overhead transparency of the fishbone diagram.*
- *Fill in the issue or problem on the right side and either present four–six causal categories, or elicit them from the group. Ask pairs or table groups to brainstorm causes. As pairs or groups share their ideas, place the item on the 'fishbone' of the causal category. Continue this procedure for several minutes until the group has a sense of the process.*

MONITORING:

As groups are working, monitor for balanced participation and group engagement. Ensure that the brainstorming stages are nonjudgmental and generative. Curtail anecdotes and explanation at this point.

MEDIATING:

Push the group thinking for additional or inventive causes. Use your inquiry skills to explore 'what if' and 'what else'.

FUTURES WHEEL

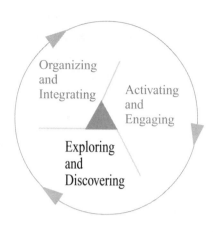

GROUP DEVELOPMENT

THIS STRATEGY IS based on diverse, creative and inventive thinking. This type of thinking tends to be low risk for novice groups. For more expert groups, the Futures Wheel offers the opportunity to stretch their thinking, breaking free of any predetermined patterns or routinized behaviors.

ATTENTION TO TASK:

The Futures Wheel process results in a basis for study groups or task forces. The ideas that are generated can be used by planning teams to explore possible policy changes, or to brainstorm options for future directions.

ATTENTION TO PROCESS:

The Futures Wheel focuses a group's creative energies and embraces the most diverse ideas. The generative process increases inclusion of all members and all perspectives.

ATTENTION TO RELATIONSHIP:

The most effective application of this strategy requires many different voices, ideas and perspectives. Group members have the freedom to entertain many different futures and to get to know each other better along the way.

MOVING ALONG THE DEVELOPMENTAL CONTINUUM

AS THE GROUP DEVELOPS YOU MIGHT EXPECT TO SEE/HEAR:

* *intentional pauses between steps to be sure everyone is included and agrees before moving on*
* *group members extending their thinking, moving past the first few ideas before adding to their chart*

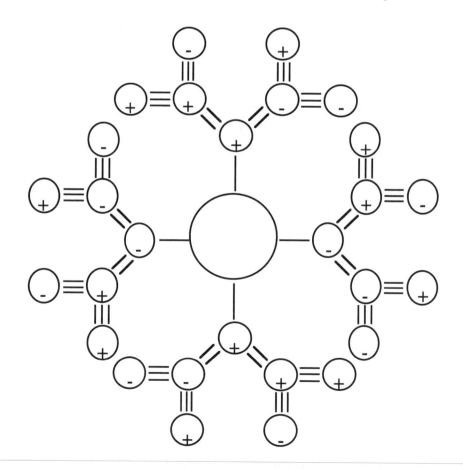

FUTURES WHEEL

THE FUTURES WHEEL is a graphic tool for forecasting ripple effects resulting from an innovation or from a disaster. It is based on the notion that any event has both positive and negative ripple effects. The aftermath of a natural disaster is an excellent case in point. The physical destruction creates many ongoing negative effects on the environment and on people's lives. Often though, building codes are reexamined and rewritten based on what scientists and engineers learn by examining the wreckage. The Futures Wheel is an excellent launching point for study groups or task forces.

Managing:

- *Form work groups of 4–6 participants.*
- *Prepare a futures wheel worksheet for each participant (see blackline master) or provide a sheet of chart paper to each group to create its own large version.*
- *Use an overhead transparency of the worksheet while giving directions to model the process.*

TIME:
Approximately 30–45 minutes

GROUPING:
4–6 participants per task group

MATERIALS:
Overhead transparency and
  worksheets of the Futures
  Wheel, chart paper, markers
  and masking tape

p. 140

Instructions to Facilitator

To apply this tool to a task, innovation, or project, use the graphic organizer, as follows:
1. Write the name of the event or innovation in the center of the wheel.
2. Work outward to the first layer of circles. Notice that there are two negatives and two positives. Emphasize that the negatives and the positives should be as diverse as possible from one another.
3. Now proceed to the second layer. Notice that each negative and each positive leads to its own negative and positive ripple effect.
4. Move outward to the third layer in a similar manner. Participants are often surprised at the possible positive and negative effects at the third layer.
5. Depending on the topic, group members can now explore possible changes in policy or brainstorm options that might thrive in the new environment.

Modeling:

This is a complex strategy that requires a variety of group skills, including task persistence and thinking flexibility. Choose a topic that will be interesting to the group, but not one that is likely to be emotionally charged. Using an overhead transparency, work through the first ring of positives and negatives. Be sure to emphasize the need for a wide difference between them. Take one set of positives and negatives and work through to the third ring, eliciting responses from the group.

Monitoring:

Move around the room visiting the work groups, especially as they fill in their first ring, checking for understanding of the process directions as well as diversity between items. Encourage group members to check for agreement before the recorder enters anything onto their Futures Wheel. Intervene as needed to ensure balanced participation.

Mediating:

Encourage group members to check for agreement before the recorder enters anything onto their Futures Wheel. Intervene as needed to ensure balanced participation. Where appropriate, ask questions or offer ideas to stretch thinking and to promote the search for novel ideas.

Variation/Application

- *Have partners create their own wheel; then work with a larger group of six to eight participants to combine their thinking.*

HERE'S WHAT! SO WHAT? NOW WHAT?

Organizing and Integrating

Activating and Engaging

Exploring and Discovering

GROUP DEVELOPMENT

HERE'S WHAT!/SO WHAT?/NOW WHAT? provides novice groups with a structure for increasing complex thinking about a topic, perspective, or data point. It also provides structure for more skillful groups to take a small sample or concrete idea and elaborate, extend and explore it.

ATTENTION TO TASK:

The simple format makes a highly effective scaffold for productivity. A large variety of ideas can be explored in a minimum amount of time.

ATTENTION TO PROCESS:

Working in pairs balances participation and increases the individual responsibility of each group member to participate and think together. Labeling a specific cognitive process at each stage focuses and enhances thinking for individuals and groups.

ATTENTION TO RELATIONSHIP:

Working in pairs makes it safe to be unsure or to share a controversial or diverse idea. Pairs have the opportunity to explore alternative perspectives as they listen and inquire into each other's thinking.

MOVING ALONG THE DEVELOPMENTAL CONTINUUM

AS THE GROUP DEVELOPS, YOU MIGHT EXPECT TO SEE AND HEAR:

* *partners pushing their thinking; exploring a wider array of possibilities*
* *an increasing number of Here's What! ideas being generated and explored within the same time frame*

HERE'S WHAT!	SO WHAT?	NOW WHAT?
24% of our grade nine students are not ready for algebra	*We have low expectations for some students* *Our K–8 program is inconsistent, different students get different messages* *Our program works for many kids*	*We need to align our K–8 curriculum, instructional practices and assessments* *Our grade nine math offerings need some adjustments* *We need to develop a summer math program between grades eight and nine to get kids ready*

HERE'S WHAT! SO WHAT? NOW WHAT?

H ERE'S WHAT! So WHAT? Now What? is a highly versatile strategy which focuses attention and energy on a specific fact, data point or idea (Here's What!). It also supports and builds capacity to surface and organize prior knowledge, interpretations and perspectives (So What?); as well as generate implications and predictions (Now What?).

MANAGING:

* *Establish pairs or trios.*
* *Distribute the 3-column worksheets.*

INSTRUCTIONS TO FACILITATOR

1. Explain the function of each column to group members. The Here's What! column is filled with specific facts or information (data), the So What? column is an interpretation of the data, and the Now What? column can be a prediction, an implication or a question for further study.
2. Provide specific Here's What items for group consideration; e.g., 40% of Grade 7 students did X. Or, ask individuals or pairs to generate a Here's What! For example, a reflection about a specific experience or a significant idea relating to the topic.
3. In pairs, or as a small table group, participants complete the So What? and Now What columns.
4. After a designated amount of time, engage in full group dialogue.

TIME:
Approximately 30 minutes

GROUPING:
Pairs or trios

MATERIALS:
3-column worksheets for each participant;
overhead transparency for modeling directions

p. 141

MODELING:

Be ready with clear and specific Here's What! examples. Elaborate one, illustrating each column and illuminating the expected thinking required for each category; e.g., generation, (Here's What!), interpretation (So What?) and prediction or implication (Now What?).

MONITORING:

Because work time is intentionally short, closely monitor progress and support facilitation of task completion. Offer a one-minute-to-end-time warning.

MEDIATING:

Orchestrate full group sharing after the completion of each column. Direct learners to create, or go on to, additional Here's What!'s as time allows.

VARIATIONS/APPLICATIONS

* *Provide the Here's What!. Have pairs or table groups process the So What? and Now What?. You might offer different Here's What! variations to each group to enrich the full group discussion. Structure the task as an opportunity to purposefully apply listening and paraphrasing skills while completing the So What? and Now What? columns.*
* *Have group members generate a Here's What! based on their observations of a data set or student work samples.*

IDEA, CATEGORY AND WEB

GROUP DEVELOPMENT

FOR NOVICE GROUPS, Idea, Category and Web scaffolds complex cognitive tasks with step-by-step directions for each stage. The hands-on chart work provides a focus for group attention and energy. Both beginning groups and those with greater expertise benefit from the opportunity to invite multiple viewpoints, and to visit and borrow from the thinking of other task groups in the walk-about stage.

ATTENTION TO TASK:

This strategy produces a large amount of organized information in a relatively short amount of time. Developing several broad categories effectively scaffolds the complexity of problem identification, supports planning, and facilitates subsequent written communication.

ATTENTION TO PROCESS:

The visual, hands-on elements required to produce the webs provides focus and engagement for working groups. The distinct stages make it possible to focus on a specific cognitive process, and provides a sense of completion, as the group finishes one stage and is ready to move to the next.

ATTENTION TO RELATIONSHIP:

This strategy combines the best of small and full group thinking. While much of the initial work is done with table groups, the final work products become the culmination of the full group's efforts. The walk-about stage fosters appreciation for the similarities and the differences in thinking and contributes to the cohesiveness of the group.

MOVING ALONG THE DEVELOPMENTAL CONTINUUM

AS THE GROUP DEVELOPS, YOU MIGHT EXPECT TO SEE/HEAR:

* *frequent use of paraphrase, and checking for agreement before items are recorded on the chart*
* *a group check for readiness and any additional ideas before moving on to develop new categories*

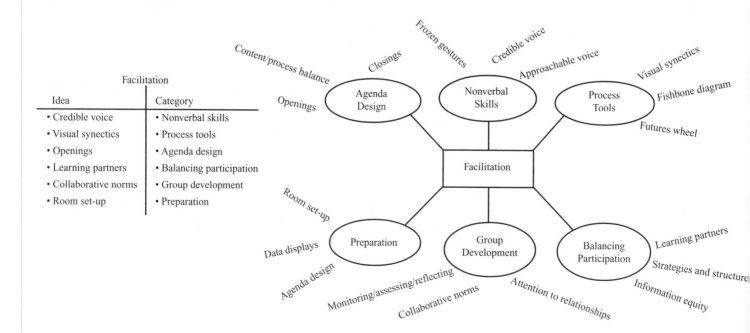

IDEA, CATEGORY AND WEB

I DEA, CATEGORY AND WEB builds on the classic strategies of brainstorming and visual organizers to extend and organize a group's thinking. Because brainstorming is both a generative and associative thinking process, group's tend to follow chains of ideas. Each idea triggers associations and relationships. In many cases, the chains run out of links and group energy falters. This strategy counteracts that problem by alternating generation and categorization, continually forcing new ideas by shifting cognitive processes.

MANAGING:

- *Prepare a T-chart. Label the columns Idea and Category.*
- *Organize task groups of 4–6 participants.*
- *Provide chart paper and markers for each group.*

TIME
30–45 minutes

GROUPING
4–6 participants per task group

MATERIALS
Chart paper and markers

p. 142

INSTRUCTIONS TO FACILITATOR

1. Share the task overhead with the group for a general idea of the structure of this strategy.
2. Model the strategy with the full group before directing groups to work independently.
3. Model with the full group as follows:
   a. Prepare a T-chart. Label the columns idea and category.
   b. Present a topic for idea and category generation. Ask group members to work with a partner for several minutes to share ideas and possible categories.
   c. Call on a group member to offer an idea. Record it in the Idea column.
   d. Generate a category label. Have either the individual who offered the idea or another participant propose a category within which the idea fits. Record it in the Category column.
        Note: Each category may be used only once. The goal is to generate broad categories for elaboration during the webbing phase.
   e. Continue the process. Develop six to twelve idea/category pairs. This is usually enough for a rich web.
   f. On a separate piece of chart paper, draw a web diagram, placing the topic in the center, with each category branching out from it.
   g. Add details to the web for at least one category.
4. Using the overhead transparency of the task directions, and a different topic, direct groups to apply the process on their own.
5. After a designated amount of time, conduct a Walk-About (or Re-Con Mission), sending task groups to view other group's work and then bring back interesting ideas to extend their own work.

MODELING:

Idea, Category and Web is a multi-stage, fairly complex strategy. The strategy description above is based on a "direct-instruction" model. That is, it assumes that the facilitator will model the full strategy with the full group. For this stage, use a topic that is familiar, fun and not related to the work topic to follow. Some examples include things that come in pairs, planning a family vacation, or San Francisco (or any large city).

MONITORING:

As you observe task groups, watch and listen for balanced participation, full group engagement and the application of appropriate verbal and non-verbal skills. Monitor and intervene if groups make premature transitions, or quick decisions that do not include all group members. Guide the process to be sure groups are working on the directed task at each stage.

MEDIATING:

Given the multi-step nature of this strategy, encourage groups to maximize their use of time, without moving too quickly and potentially missing important ideas or categories. Use your inquiry skills to facilitate thinking beyond the surface. As groups are creating their webs, support extension and elaboration of ideas within each category.

INTERRELATIONSHIP DIAGRAM

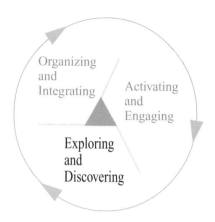

Organizing and Integrating

Activating and Engaging

Exploring and Discovering

GROUP DEVELOPMENT

INTERRELATIONSHIP DIAGRAMS reveal critical relationships among the elements in a system. For novice groups the process illuminates a big picture view of the system. For more expert groups, the process reveals surprises regarding unanticipated causes and effects.

ATTENTION TO TASK:

This tool directs and coordinates a planning team's decision-making conversations. By engaging in rich and focused dialogue regarding key drivers in the system, groups can determine starting points for improvement plans, choices regarding resource allocation and communication needs within and outside the system.

ATTENTION TO PROCESS:

The visual nature of this tool provides a focusing third point for group dialogue. As the group determines which factors are causes and which effects, each step in the process creates increased understanding.

ATTENTION TO RELATIONSHIP:

This tool requires a collaborative effort and is most effective when implemented by a group with a variety of roles and experiences. The visual focus and structured process produces a conversation that engages group members in sharing their own perspectives and being open to considering others. Ultimately, group members learn more about the system, each other and themselves.

MOVING ALONG THE DEVELOPMENTAL CONTINUUM

AS THE GROUP DEVELOPS, YOU MIGHT EXPECT TO SEE/HEAR:

* *increasing checking for and clarifying of assumptions*
* *a balance between individual advocacy for an idea and inquiry into other's ideas*
* *group members dealing constructively with conflicting ideas*

Interrelationship Diagram: Student Mathematics Achievement

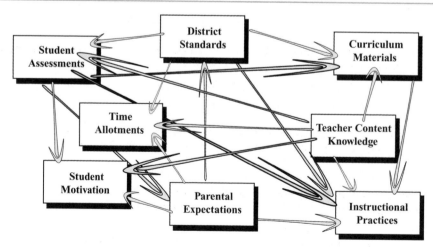

Drivers	Effects
• District Standards	• Instructional Practices
• Teacher content knowledge	• Time allotments
• Parental expectations	• Student motivation
• Student assessments	• Curriculum materials

INTERRELATIONSHIP DIAGRAM

INTERRELATIONSHIP DIAGRAMS help groups to see important relationships within problems, processes, and systems. This tool and the creation of the diagrams map out logical but not always apparent connections between related elements. It helps groups to see and decide what elements within the problem, process or system are the major causes or drivers and what elements are the effects. The initial work can often be messy. It is best to regard this as a drafting process, with final clean drafts crafted at the end if a graphic representation is needed to communicate findings to others.

MANAGING:

- *Organize groups of 4–8 participants.*
- *Create stations for each work group using chart stands or posting chart paper on the wall. Provision each station with chart paper, markers and masking tape.*

TIME:
30–45 minutes

GROUPING:
4–8 participants per task group

MATERIALS:
Overhead transparency of task directions; completed interrelationship diagram.

pp. 143–145

INSTRUCTIONS TO THE FACILITATOR

1. Introduce participants to the concept of seeking and separating causes or drivers from effects. For example, a high level of parental support (driver) is most likely going to produce high achievement for their children (effect).
2. Direct group to select a problem, process or system to explore. Suggest they choose something they are presently working with, or something they feel is particularly relevant to them.
3. Group members brainstorm a list of the major categories of issues related to the selected topic. Note: Hold the number of categories to six to eight. More than this can be difficult to manage.

 Facilitator's Tip: For novice groups, you might want to use a strategy such as Brainstorm and Pass to structure the brainstorming process.

4. Group members arrange the names of the major categories randomly in a circle around a sheet of chart paper. They can write directly on the chart paper or use sticky notes that can be rearranged if needed during the drafting process.
5. Selecting one category as a starting point, group members ask two-way questions to determine whether this category is a driver or an effect of each of the other categories. They draw arrows from the drivers to the effects. This process continues through each of the categories.
6. After all of the categories have been addressed, groups count the number of arrows going away from each category. These are the drivers. They rank the drivers from highest to lowest in impact. Be sure to emphasize that there can never be two-headed arrows. The group must decide which category dominates the other.
7. Finally, group members count the number of arrows pointing towards each category and rank the effects from highest to lowest in terms of the major outcomes of the current problem, process or system.
8. Individual groups, or the full group studies the results and considers intervention points that will amplify desired results and minimize less desirable outcomes.

MODELING:

Use an overhead transparency of a completed interrelationship chart to demonstrate the anticipated result of the process (see Blackline Masters).
Using the example, emphasize that the categories should be broad and diverse.

MONITORING:

As groups are working, move around the room checking to be sure the recorder or a small sub-set of the task group is not dominating the interaction. Encourage pausing before arrows are drawn, to be sure there is understanding and agreement.

MEDIATING:

It is important that working groups have a shared understanding of each category. Engage with small groups, probing for some examples that illustrate their various categories. Inquire, also about differences between categories.
Occasionally poll groups to describe their thinking about some of the choices on the chart. For example, "I see you're indicating that _____ is a driver for _____; what's your thinking about that?"

VARIATION/APPLICATION

- *Interrelationship Diagrams are an effective process for determining the causes for the Fishbone/Cause-Effect Diagrams tool. Once the Interrelationship Diagram is complete, transfer the identified drivers to the skeleton of the Fishbone.*

INTER-VENN-TION

Organizing and Integrating

Activating and Engaging

Exploring and Discovering

GROUP DEVELOPMENT

INTER-VENN-TION creates a psychologically safe opportunity for cognitively complex conversations. For both novice and expert groups, this strategy supports exploration of a variety of topics and builds understanding and relationship. Intentional use of short time frames maximizes participation and task focus.

ATTENTION TO TASK:

The Inter-VENN-tion pattern of one to two to four is inclusive, offers both thinking and speaking time for all members, and builds understanding and/or agreement in a time-efficient manner. A maximum amount of interaction can be accomplished in a minimum amount of time, furthering group development, as well as task focus.

ATTENTION TO PROCESS:

The first step in this process structures individual work and provides some think time. The remainder of the process draws from and builds on the individual member's experiences and perspectives. This combination encompasses productive learning opportunities for different working styles and balances participation, providing time for deep exploration of the topic at hand.

ATTENTION TO RELATIONSHIP:

The me-map information and the expanding participation process provides a safe opportunity for actively questioning and exploring individual and collective thinking.

MOVING ALONG THE DEVELOPMENTAL CONTINUUM

AS THE GROUP DEVELOPS, YOU MIGHT EXPECT TO SEE/HEAR:

* *group members giving their full attention to each other, listening without interruption*
* *groups managing their time to complete the task within the timeframe*

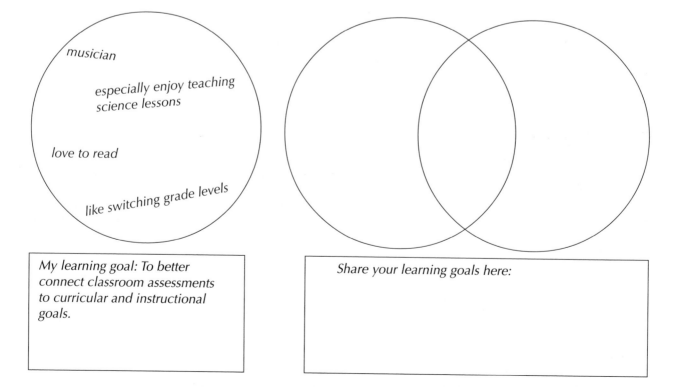

musician

especially enjoy teaching science lessons

love to read

like switching grade levels

My learning goal: To better connect classroom assessments to curricular and instructional goals.

Share your learning goals here:

INTER-VENN-TION

I NTER-VENN-TION is a four-step strategy that follows the pattern of individual to small group work (one to four participants). This strategy is effective for building relationships as groups are forming. It is also useful for finding common ground about a new initiative or school improvement plan.

MANAGING:

Provide Inter-VENN-tion worksheets for each participant.

INSTRUCTIONS TO FACILITATOR

1. Individual Me-Maps. For this step, participants work on their own. Ask them to draw a circle and fill the inside with words or short phrases about themselves and/or their work life. They might include likes, dislikes, special experiences, favorite leisure activities, things about their family and family life, as well as job information, satisfactions, challenges, etc. Model one about yourself on a large chart paper as you describe the task.

 Facilitator's Tip: To save work time, the individual work on the Me-Maps can be done prior to the meeting.

2. Partner-Up. Organize the group into pairs (e.g., eye contact partners, elbow partners, or one of your favorite pairing strategies).
3. Create a VENN. As they explore and discover their similarities and differences, pairs create and complete a VENN diagram, placing the information in the appropriate areas. Invite group members to add new information as it comes up during their discussion. Notice that they will sometimes have to create categories to organize their similarities.
4. Pairs Squared. Each pair finds another pair and partners introduce and tell a little bit about each other. (Be sure you let the group know they will be doing this prior to forming quartets, so they can prepare).

TIME:
20–30 minutes

GROUPING:
Individuals participants; then pairs

MATERIALS:
Overhead transparency of both blank and completed worksheets.

pp. 146–147

MODELING:

As part of your directions, provide several examples for the me-map. When the topic is appropriate, create your own me-map as an example.

MONITORING:

When partners are working, monitor for balanced participation. Provide a time cue to be sure that each partner has had a chance to share information, and that both are ready for the cross-introduction step.

MEDIATING:

Remind group members that they can add information as they work on their Venn Diagrams.

VARIATIONS/APPLICATIONS

- *Inter-VENN-tion is an effective strategy for any topic. For example, participants can individually complete a 'me-map' for pros and cons about an initiative, attributes of the ideal classroom, or satisfactions and challenges implementing a specific program. Then, pairs create their Venn diagram.*
- *This strategy is effective for developing and sharing personal learning or program-based goals. Start by having individuals include a goal in their me-maps. Then, be sure to have them share their goals as part of the introductions in quartets. Let them know you will be collecting key goals from quartets as part of the full-group sharing.*

MATCHBOOK DEFINITIONS

GROUP DEVELOPMENT

THE SHORT TIME allotment for creating Matchbook Definitions creates a high level of interdependence and task focus. For both skillful and novice groups it is a quick way to capture complex or abstract ideas with simple, fundamental, useable language.

ATTENTION TO TASK:

When there is a need for agreement on language, a large group, divided into smaller working groups can generate some initial language that can be synthesized and refined at a later stage. Use Matchbook Definitions to scaffold agreement on definitions of abstract concepts, such as excellence, achievement or professional.

ATTENTION TO PROCESS:

Creates shared understanding of abstract concepts while reducing the likelihood of bogging down over language choices.

ATTENTION TO RELATIONSHIP:

The short time frame of this strategy focuses group energy and increases inclusiveness. There is a need for all group members to contribute their ideas, and little time for wordsmithing.

MOVING ALONG THE DEVELOPMENTAL CONTINUUM

AS THE GROUP DEVELOPS, YOU MIGHT EXPECT TO SEE/HEAR:

- *greater attention to including all ideas and everyone's contributions*
- *synergistic products based on a variety of group members ideas*

Notes

MATCHBOOK DEFINITIONS

MATCHBOOK DEFINITIONS uses the effect of a short time frame to focus a group's energy on synthesizing potentially complex concepts. It is particularly useful for organizing and integrating content after input or study.

MANAGING:

- *Make ready a sheet of chart paper (you may want to use half sheets) and one or two markers for each table group.*
- *Organize table groups of 4–6 participants.*

TIME:
15 minutes (with 4–5 minutes of production time).

GROUPING:
4–6 participants per task group

MATERIALS:
Full or half sheets of chart paper, markers, masking tape.

INSTRUCTIONS TO FACILITATOR

1. Describe the nature and quality of a "matchbook" definition—succinct, brief, capturing the essence of a concept.
2. Inform the group that they will be crafting a 10–12 word definition of the term or concept being explored, that succinctly captures the essence of the idea, in a brief amount of time. They are to present their work on the distributed chart paper (assure them that this product is intended as a rough draft, not a polished production).
3. When time is up, invite each work group to share their Matchbook Definition.

    Note: You may want to post each chart for later reference or refinement.

 Facilitator Tip: Use a public timer to help groups self-monitor.

MODELING:

Describe clearly the critical attributes of a Matchbook Definition, as above.

MONITORING:

Because work time is intentionally short, closely monitor progress and support facilitation of task completion. Offer one-minute-to-end-time warning.

MEDIATING:

Frame the task so that groups are generating critical elements or important points about the topic.

VARIATION/APPLICATION

- *Have groups create a symbol to represent the idea or concept, rather than (or in addition to) using words.*

ROUND THE ROOM AND BACK AGAIN

GROUP DEVELOPMENT

THIS STRATEGY builds interdependence, enables access to the rich resource of colleagues and increases confidence for each group member by providing information pertinent to the topic under study. For novice groups, having a shared knowledge base provides a foundation for working together.

ATTENTION TO TASK:

The efficiency of producing and pooling an information bank facilitates task completion. This strategy surfaces participants' experiences and frames of reference regarding the topic under consideration.

ATTENTION TO PROCESS:

Participation in this strategy provides a safe risk for many individuals, providing everyone with a baseline of shared information.

ATTENTION TO RELATIONSHIP:

Relationships are built and reinforced when individual's ideas are validated and extended through interaction with colleagues.

MOVING ALONG THE DEVELOPMENTAL CONTINUUM

AS THE GROUP DEVELOPS, YOU MIGHT EXPECT TO SEE/HEAR:

* *increasing efficiency in moving around the room to interact with group members*
* *increasing confidence in sharing, seeking and retaining ideas*

Notes

ROUND THE ROOM AND BACK AGAIN

R OUND THE ROOM AND BACK AGAIN engages group member's previous knowledge and experience, as well as their energy. This simple strategy is effective for transitions between topics or when introducing a new one. Consider using this strategy instead of a formal break. It provides a physical stretch when time is tight and you need to move the agenda forward.

MANAGING:

- *Organize tables groups of 3–6 participants.*
- *Each participant will need note paper.*

INSTRUCTIONS TO FACILITATOR:

1. Have each participant take out a sheet of paper and write one example of the topic the group is about to explore. (e.g., name one source of data that you use beyond norm-referenced test scores.)
2. Individuals then set aside their writing materials and on the facilitator's direction move around the room sharing their examples and listening to the examples of others. The challenge is to rely only on auditory memory.
3. Time is called after about two minutes, or as people's memory banks fill up (seven items, plus or minus two). Individuals then return to their seats and write down as many examples as they can recall.
4. Table groups then pool their examples and extend their lists.

TIME:
15 minutes (about 3 minutes for initial auditory collection)

GROUPING:
3–6 participants per task group

MATERIALS:
Note paper

p. 148

MODELING:

Give a clear example of an item that would be appropriate for this strategy. The items should be short, succinct and easy to remember. Examples include various data sources, qualities of an effective literacy program, criteria for assigning grades, or effective resources for hands-on science instruction.

MONITORING:

Timing is sensitive in this strategy. You want to provide enough time for gathering multiple items, but not so much that people become overloaded. You might inquire randomly to determine how many items individuals have collected. Five to seven is about right.

MEDIATING:

Be clear that the focus is on idea generation, not elaboration. The goal is to develop an extensive, shared list of information, examples, or ideas related to a topic.

VARIATIONS/APPLICATIONS

- *Have table groups extend their pooled information bank.*
- *Have table groups compare/contrast their lists to an expert source, such as a hand-out or previously prepared list.*
- *Have table groups categorize their information banks.*
- *Collect examples from each table to create a full group master list.*

SAY SOMETHING

Organizing and Integrating

Activating and Engaging

Exploring and Discovering

GROUP DEVELOPMENT

FOR NOVICE GROUPS, partnered structures provide a psychologically safe way to build relationship and focus on potentially difficult-to-discuss topics. For more skillful groups, pairs can accelerate shared understanding. Combining partners creates a foundation for larger group configurations ready to tackle cognitively and emotionally complex tasks.

ATTENTION TO TASK:

This strategy focuses group members on information relevant to the task at hand. It is effective in providing a starting point for more extended conversations.

ATTENTION TO PROCESS:

As with all partnered work, this strategy balances participation and provides a time-effective method for exploring information. The small group and brief time frame makes this strategy useful for considering emotionally charged topics.

ATTENTION TO RELATIONSHIP:

The structured exchange facilitates sharing of ideas, perspectives, and understanding. Often, a highlight or important point for one partner illuminates new ways of thinking for the other and vice versa.

MOVING ALONG THE DEVELOPMENTAL CONTINUUM

AS THE GROUP DEVELOPS, YOU MIGHT EXPECT TO SEE/HEAR:

- *succinct presentation of ideas in a brief amount of time*
- *increasing focus on the task*
- *partners purposeful elaboration on each other's ideas*
- *shifting from task completion to broadening understanding as the goal*

Notes

SAY SOMETHING

S AY SOMETHING is a paired reading strategy developed by Egawa and Harste (2001) for constructing meaning from text-based information. Through structured exchanges, group members develop relationships between new information and what they already know or believe. This thinking out loud, supported by attentive listening, enhances individual and shared understandings.

MANAGING:

- *Identify an appropriate piece of text or other focusing material. Prepare a copy for each group member.*
- *Establish partners.*

TIME:
Varies depending on the reading.
    Generally 15–20 minutes.
GROUPING:
Pairs

INSTRUCTIONS TO FACILITATOR

1. Identify the text and the stopping points, or have partners look over a piece of text and decide together how far they will read silently before stopping to say something.
2. Describe the nature of the interactions, explaining that the something might be a question, a brief summary, a key point, an interesting idea or a new connection.
3. Once each partner has reached the chosen stopping point, both partners exchange comments, or say something.
4. Partners continue the process until the selection is completed.
5. After a designated amount of time, engage the whole group in a discussion of the text.

MATERIALS:
A reading selection for each
    participant. An overhead
    transparency timer.

p. 149

MODELING:

When giving the directions, provide one or two examples of appropriate say somethings. These should be succinct, thoughtful and related the text.

MONITORING:

The time frame for this strategy is intentionally brief. It is effective to post a public timer displaying the full time allotment, so partners can determine how long to converse, and how quickly to move on to the next reading.

MEDIATING:

To focus the paired interactions, or to stimulate a specific type of thinking, the facilitator may want to provide a say something stem for completion. For example, "one connection to my work is . . .", or "a question that comes to mind when I read this is . . ." Use the same stem, or provide variation for each stopping point.

VARIATIONS/APPLICATIONS

- *Say Something can be focused around a variety of products, such as student work samples, homework assignments, or data sets.*
- *Use trios, rather than pairs, for more perspectives, or if the group has an uneven number.*
- *Key Concepts/Key Ideas is a variant of Say Something. It works in a similar pattern, but participants read the entire selection first (rather than designated sections) highlighting points of interest. Then, partners alternate turns sharing their comments and responding.*

SYNECTICS—FOUR BOX

Organizing and Integrating

Activating and Engaging

Exploring and Discovering

GROUP DEVELOPMENT

SYNECTICS supports novice groups by engaging members with each other and with tough-to-talk-about topics. The four-box organizer provides a focus, or third point, for reference and idea generation. For skillful groups, this strategy sustains and expands thinking by opening frames of reference and inviting divergent perspectives.

ATTENTION TO TASK:

This strategy focuses group attention on the topic under consideration, as well as efficiently surfacing underlying issues, attitudes and understandings.

ATTENTION TO PROCESS:

The brainstorming process supports creative idea development. Brainstorming requires two critical protocols: Accepting all offerings without judgment, and separating idea generation from elaboration and clarification.
Productive groups increase their flexibility by developing a repertoire of metaphorical thinking tools such as Four Box Synectics.

ATTENTION TO RELATIONSHIP:

The open-ended quality of this strategy reduces right/wrong dynamics, inviting participation by all members. Opportunities to hear everyone's ideas develop an appreciation for the mind styles of others. Experiences such as this increase respect for multiple points of view and the power of productive humor to diffuse potential tensions.

MOVING ALONG THE DEVELOPMENTAL CONTINUUM

AS THE GROUP DEVELOPS, YOU MIGHT EXPECT TO SEE/HEAR:

- *increasing solicitation of ideas from quieter members*
- *increasing listening and piggybacking on previous comments*
- *strategic use of creative thinking skills when groups get stuck*

FOUR BOX SYNECTICS

coffee	toast
orange juice	bacon

Teaching is like a(n)_____ coffee _____ because . . .

SYNECTICS—FOUR BOX

F OUR BOX SYNECTICS promotes metaphorical and creative thinking. This strategy applies a four-frame organizer that supports participants in quickly generating novel ideas about topics that they are about to explore. Industrial psychologists, William Gordon and George Prince coined the term Synectics by joining two Greek roots: syn—bringing together and ectics—diverse elements. They use the term to mean 'a metaphorical problem solving process' in order to 'make the familiar strange' or 'make the strange familiar'.

MANAGING:

- *Reproduce a copy of the Four-Box Synectics recording form for each table group.*
- *Organize table groups of 4–6 participants.*
- *Select a concept or topic as the focus of comparison.*

INSTRUCTIONS TO FACILITATOR

1. Determine a recorder: Some options include: numbering-off using random selection, group designee, participant volunteer, or facilitator's choice.
2. As a large group generate common labels within a category for each of the four boxes and record these on the overhead transparency master: Some options include: favorite foods, regional food specialties, regional tourist attractions or local experiences, sports or recreational activities, common household objects, or international landmarks.
3. Model an example based on one of the labels in one of the quadrants. The goal is to generate 3–4 comparisons in each of the four cells.
4. After three minutes of brainstorming, ask the group to pause. Offer another minute for each task group to choose a greatest hit from each cell to share with the full group.
5. After another minute, refocus the group for sharing.

TIME:
15–20 minutes

GROUPING:
4–6 participants per task group

MATERIALS:
1 Four-Box Synectics Recording
 Page for each table group

p. 150

MODELING:

Select one of the labels in one of the quadrants and offer an example of a synectical connection. " _____ is like ____ because . . ."

MONITORING:

Pay attention while task groups are sharing out their greatest hits. The nature of the synectic comparisons, as well as the group responses to them, offer useful information about the emotional state of the group and the relationships between and among participants.

MEDIATING:

Inserting a structured brainstorming activity prior to the synectics process scaffolds metaphorical thinking. Have task groups brainstorm lists of parts, materials, properties, functions and processes associated with the object or activity label in each quadrant. Using their lists, each table group makes associations between the objects and activities and the detailed lists of parts, materials, properties, functions and processes. Generating these elements enhances group members' capacities to produce creative connections.

Note: It is often useful to briefly review brainstorming protocols prior to beginning the process.

VARIATIONS/APPLICATIONS

- *Make it a Visual Synectics by providing an image for comparison, rather than items or categories. Give small groups a small selection of picture cards to choose from, or display one image on the overhead projector for work groups to process. Then follow steps 4–5 above.*
- *Try this process using compare and contrast: [This object or activity] is like; as well as is not like [the topic] because . . .*
- *Use Four-Box Synectics at the end of a work session to organize and integrate information and concepts.*

WALK-AROUND SURVEY

GROUP DEVELOPMENT

THE WALK-AROUND SURVEY builds skills in analyzing and generating theory from data. Novice groups benefit from an experience with data that is not threatening or emotionally charged. Skillful groups extend their expertise in working with data, especially when encouraged to generate multiple theories, using the same data sets.

ATTENTION TO TASK:

The flexibility of the categories makes this a generic tool for multiple purposes.

ATTENTION TO PROCESS:

Specific thinking skills are emphasized at each stage in this process, building capacity for data gathering and theory building.

ATTENTION TO RELATIONSHIP:

This strategy fosters group self-analysis.

MOVING ALONG THE DEVELOPMENTAL CONTINUUM

AS THE GROUP DEVELOPS, YOU MIGHT EXPECT TO SEE/HEAR:

* *deeper inquiry into the data with extending questions, such as "what else", "what haven't we thought about yet?"*
* *attention to balancing participation and eliciting ideas from all members*
* *clearer connections between the data analysis and the theory generation*

WALK-AROUND SURVEY

TOPIC _____

Effective category possibilities include: • *Positive results, negative results, interesting results* • *Key points, significant ideas, questions* • *Concerns, hopes, stumbling blocks*		

WALK-AROUND SURVEY

WALK-AROUND SURVEY is an interactive strategy that involves the full group in generating new ideas, synthesizing previously learned material or sharing present thinking and understandings. Like many other strategies designed to link and extend knowledge and experiences, it follows a diamond pattern of individual work; large-group sharing; small-group sharing and, in some cases individual work, once again.

MANAGING:

- *Establish groups of 4–6 participants.*
- *Prepare and distribute the Walk-around Survey form.*

TIME:
30–45 Minutes

GROUPING:
4–6 participants

MATERIALS:
Walk-Around Survey Forms;
Overhead transparencies of
  survey and process directions

*pp.
151,
152*

INSTRUCTIONS TO FACILITATOR

1. Individual Work. Given the Walk-Around Survey format, or worksheet and a specific topic, participants generate their own response for each category in the left-hand column of the page.
2. Full-Group Exchange. Next, participants walk around and complete their page by surveying group members for their responses. They briefly capture their colleagues' thinking, as well as their names, in each appropriate box. The name provides accountability and a potential future reference (group members can go back to the "source" for more information, or to clarify thinking).
    Process Note: Group members should not collect information from their own small groups; they will have an opportunity to exchange thinking with them later on.
3. Small-Group Processing. After 10–12 minutes, or whatever seems appropriate, participants return to their small groups. They share their collected information, as well as their own thinking.
4. Organize and Integrate. Group members explore and analyze the information they have collected (look for themes, compare and contrast the items, organize into new categories). At this stage, the small groups are analyzing their findings.
5. Generating Theory: Now ask small group to identify a particular pattern or theme in the data from which they can make a hypotheses, or generate a theory about the group. Ask each small group to share their theory, and make connections to the supporting data using a What and Why reporting pattern. (What: our theory/Why: some of our supporting data).

MODELING:

Using a transparency of the Survey Worksheet, describe the process and offer specific examples that illustrate each category.
Prepare specific examples for steps 4 (analysis) and 5 (generating theory).

MONITORING:

During the full group exchange, monitor movement, checking that participants interact with several group members in the limited time available. During the small group processing, be sure that all participants have an opportunity to share their ideas.

Facilitator's Tip: Increase task focus by using a public timer.

MEDIATING:

During the analysis stage, use your inquiry skills to extend and deepen group thinking.

VARIATIONS/APPLICATIONS

If time is limited:
- *You might reduce the number of boxes.*
- *Have group members get a bingo rather than fill in the entire matrix.*
- *Ask group members to organize their individual responses prior to arrival at the meeting.*

WINDOWS AND MIRRORS

GROUP DEVELOPMENT

Windows and Mirrors supports group members in developing increased consciousness about how individual decisions, choices and behaviors influence the group's performance as a whole.

ATTENTION TO TASK:

This strategy supports the development of criteria for group work (or any other task). As a group acknowledges and attends to its process and relationships, its task work is facilitated.

ATTENTION TO PROCESS:

In this strategy, the process is the content. As group members become increasingly conscious about their process skills, they are better able to adjust and modify their behaviors moving increasingly toward expertise.

ATTENTION TO RELATIONSHIP:

As above with process, this strategy is designed to call attention to the group members' relationships and provide a venue for describing, discussing and improving them.

MOVING ALONG THE DEVELOPMENTAL CONTINUUM

AS THE GROUP DEVELOPS, YOU MIGHT EXPECT TO SEE/HEAR:

- *increasing comfort with silence and longer pauses between speakers*
- *eliciting participation from quiet group members*
- *paraphrasing of previous comments prior to adding thoughts*

WINDOW

Imagine you are observing a group struggling as it works with data. Group members are:

> *Off-task*

> *Unfocused*

> *Unproductive*

What specifically do you see/hear?

MIRROR

Imagine you are in a special, mirrored meeting room where you can observe your reflection.

What do you see yourself doing to help the group focus, hear one another and support the development of shared understanding?

WINDOWS AND MIRRORS

WINDOWS AND MIRRORS provides a psychologically safe way for a group to gain insights into their own process and relationship skills. This strategy uses visualization to force group members to take an outside, or third position, describing what they might see through a window, or reflected in a mirror.

MANAGING:

- *Organize table groups of 6–8 participants representing a variety of roles and perspectives.*
- *Create overhead transparencies or charts related to the topic at hand.*

TIME
Approximately 20–30 minutes

GROUPING:
6–8 participants per task group

MATERIALS:
Task overhead, note paper, chart paper

INSTRUCTIONS TO FACILITATOR

1. Determine a recorder for each small group (use first name beginning closest to A or your favorite strategy). You might have recorders create a T-chart labeled See on one side; Hear on the other.
2. Direct task groups to imagine that they are viewing a particular scenario through a special one-way window. For example, you might ask for a description of a group that is struggling with data work.

 Facilitator's Tip: Be sure to request specific, observable behaviors (what they might see and hear).

3. Ask recorders to report out some of the items on each group's list. You may find it useful to create a master chart.
4. Now, ask the groups to imagine that they are in a special room in which they can observe their own behavior reflected in mirrored walls. Ask, "what do you see yourself doing that makes a difference for this group?" For example, given the scenario above, you might ask what each sees him/herself doing to focus the group and increase its effectiveness. Follow the same process (recorders capture specific, observable behaviors).
5. Once both the windows and mirrors lists have been shared (and charted) ask the group a variety of process questions designed to surface insights and goals regarding the topic focus.

MODELING:

Use a T-chart to model examples of observable behaviors; specifically what might be seen and heard through the window or mirror.

MONITORING:

Listen for balanced contributions to each of the lists. You might want to structure the sharing to balance participation. Be sure the items are observable and specific.

MEDIATING:

Use visualization techniques to engage the group's energy in imagining the scenarios. You might describe the room, the number of participants, what's on the walls, the seating configuration, etc.

VARIATIONS/APPLICATIONS

Analyze any gaps between a group's own process and relationship skills and the standard to which they aspire, including:
- *skillful facilitation; effective meetings; collaborative cultures.*

Notes

CHAPTER SIX—Leading Systems: Structures and Capacities for Continuous School Improvement

"The biochemist Lawrence Henderson was influential through his early use of the term "system" to denote both living organisms and social systems. From that time on, a system has come to mean an integrated whole whose essential properties arise from the relationship between its parts, and "systems thinking" the understanding of a phenomenon within the context of a larger whole. This is, in fact the root meaning of the word "system," which derives from the Greek *synhistanai* ("to place together"). To understand things systematically literally means to put them into a context, to establish the nature of their relationships."

—Fritjof Capra

SYSTEMS INFRASTRUCTURE

School improvement requires thinking at the systems level. The parts only matter in relation to the whole. Leading systems requires ongoing attention to these interrelationships and to communicating these interactions to others in the organization who are working on their specific parts. Without a systems lens and purposeful connection making among participants, isolated efforts often lack impact or at worst, unaligned initiatives undermine each other.

The processes of data-driven dialogue and collaborative inquiry organize the essential structures and capacities for comprehensive organizational development. Each structure and capacity has its own integrity and is a vital subsystem of the greater map (see Figure 6.1).

Two interlocking elements, *Leading Systems* and *Clear and Agreed Upon Standards* frame the territory, illustrating that true standards express themselves at the systems level. These are the qualities and expectations we hold in common for ourselves and for others. Without a systems view and systems thinking, standards become wishful thinking or inspirationally vague goals for a select few.

LEADING SYSTEMS

The ability to see the systems that produce and sustain high quality learning is a vital resource for individuals, teams and organizations. This perspective requires a shift in thinking from seeing parts to seeing wholes, for it is the whole of the experience that educates students. Without such a lens we send students from a lesson on nutrition to a

Figure 6.1: Leading Systems

Leading Systems

Technological Infrastructure: *How we know*

Managing Data

- Identifying
- Organizing
- Accessing
- Displaying

Organizational and Individual Capacities: *What we talk about*

Structural Capacities

- Aligned curriculum
- Aligned instruction
- Aligned assessments

Technical Capacities

- Assessment literacy
- Data analysis skills
- Learning-focused instruction
- Learning-focused supervision
- Learning-focused professional development
- Standards-based grading/reporting

Professional Capacities

- Knowledge of the structure of the content discipline(s)
- Knowledge of Self (values, beliefs, standards)
- Knowledge of teaching skills and strategies
- Knowledge of learners and learning

Sociological Infrastructure: *How and why we talk*

Attention to Task

- Learning-focused
- Time and energy efficient
- Data-driven

Attention to Process

- Shared tools and structures
- Learning-focused conversations
- Data-driven dialogue

Attention to Relationship

- Shared norms and values
- School culture
- Professional community

Clear and Agreed Upon Standards

Copyright © 2004 MiraVia, LLC • Laura Lipton & Bruce Wellman, Co-Directors

cafeteria stocked with soft drink machines and french fries and then out to raise funds for improving the school playground by selling candy bars.

Lacking a systems lens we have one view of what matters for student learning and a radically different view of what matters to support the learning of the adults who teach those students (Lipton and Wellman, 2001). A more comprehensive lens helps leaders develop philosophically congruent approaches throughout the organization.

Systems produce learning. Horizontally across the day and vertically across the years, learning is the cumulative effect of experiences that meld with developing minds to shape human learners and learning outcomes. There must be vertical articulation and alignment from grade to grade. This is as true within an individual department as it is between departments. The English department and the Social Studies department need to be on the same page when it comes to student writing. Macrocurriculum for cognitive and behavioral skills must permeate all areas of the school system.

This aspect of systems thinking requires a temporal view. Individuals and organizations need to learn to see across time and learn to plan and implement improvement efforts and interventions over monthly and yearly spans. Major program changes or interventions for particular types of learners can take years to accomplish. Without wider temporal horizons, school personnel are caught in the demands of the moment, blind to potential signs of progress.

Further, viewing through a systems lens reveals patterns and processes in all aspects of the organization. Studying patterns of human interaction provides essential information. What people talk about and how they talk to one another comprises the core of the relational underpinnings of the organization. Ultimately, data use is institutionalized as part of the patterns that create and sustain the system.

Systems and systems thinking are also built by understanding processes. While structures and routines are important, how people go about their activities develops the living system that binds people to one another and to the organization's values and goals.

The first conclusion is that those outside the system with responsibility for articulating a program for reform have nothing resembling a holistic conception of the system they seek to influence. In principle, I have argued that ignorance need not be lethal, although it almost always has been. The second conclusion is that being part of the system—part so to speak, of the school culture—in no way guarantees that one understands the system in any comprehensive way.

—Seymour B. Sarason

CLEAR AND AGREED UPON STANDARDS

Standards come in many forms, shapes and sizes. What matters most for productive systems growth and development is that all significant stakeholders agree on those standards that have the greatest significance for the organization and for those whom the organization serves. To support steady improvements in student learning results, the organization and all individuals that interact with the organization need to be clear about three different types of standards (Nave, Miech and Mosteller, 2000).

CONTENT STANDARDS. These standards define the subject matter that schools expect students to master. Clear standards articulate the declarative knowledge of concepts and information that support deeper understandings, the procedural knowledge that forms the ways of knowing within a discipline and the conditional knowledge of when and when not to apply rules, procedures and formulas.

PERFORMANCE STANDARDS. These standards establish criteria for judging student products and performances. They define the levels that determine mastery of a set of knowledge and skills. Performance standards also define the proportion of the student population that must meet established criteria in order for the school or school program to claim success.

OPPORTUNITY TO LEARN STANDARDS. These standards are about equity of resources within and between schools. Within schools they mean providing opportunities for all students to engage in a rich and challenging curriculum. Opportunity to learn also means that the school provides students with multiple ways to engage in meaningful learning, providing options for second chances and the supports necessary to meet learning goals. Between schools, at the district level, opportunity to learn standards require budget and program decisions that spread resources fairly among schools and target resources to areas of greatest need.

Clear and agreed upon standards are also important within the work culture of schools and districts. Expectations for adult interactions are organized by the values and beliefs within that culture. Successful collaborative teams take time to clarify these working agreements. They also take time to reflect upon their work and their ways of working (Garmston and Wellman, 1999).

The systems lens and clear standards organize three essential infrastructures that support the work of school improvement: the technological infrastructure organizes how we know the system and its results; organizational and individual capacities frame what we talk about in order to improve the system; and the sociological infrastructure frames how and why we talk together in our schools.

A systems view illuminates connections between these interacting components. Standards and their measures then become points of reference for data collection, systems analysis, problem finding and problem solving.

TECHNOLOGICAL INFRASTRUCTURE: HOW WE KNOW

Data management systems are an important resource for efficient collaborative inquiry. Effective databases link multiple sources of data, providing a variety of cross sections and interfaces. These databases ease access to exploring relationships between various data sources, e.g., student and teacher demographic information, assessment information and teacher grade books.

However, databases are only as good as the data within them. End users and technical resource people need to work together to carefully develop practical and accessible data templates to support collaborative, data-driven inquiry. Data management is mostly common sense. Straightforward spreadsheet software that creates charts and graphs facilitates the creation of visually accessible and engaging data displays.

From a systems development perspective, this arena needs to develop simultaneously with the sociological infrastructure. Collaborative processes founder if data is not readily accessible. And the data itself has little value, no matter how well displayed, if the collaborative skills of the group are not sufficiently developed to make use of that data.

ORGANIZATIONAL AND INDIVIDUAL CAPACITIES: WHAT WE TALK ABOUT

Three major capacities become the focus of conversation in improving schools: structural capacities; technical capacities; and professional capacities. We consider the term capacity as 'the ability to do something.' Practitioners, schools and districts have to continually develop these three capacities to ensure success for all students.

STRUCTURAL CAPACITIES

Curriculum, instruction and assessment systems are the center of what schools do. The work in this arena is ongoing and never ending. Each area has an ever-expanding knowledge base. The hard work at the school and district level is the work of developing sustained and focused effort within these domains. Curricula are notoriously difficult to coordinate. The paper curriculum and the delivered curriculum are often miles apart. Instruction tends to vary widely from class to class. And in the worst cases, assessments have a life of their own and are not always linked to either the curriculum or to the ways in which material is taught.

Alignment of these cultural arenas is a process, not a task. It is through dialogue and discussion organized around student information that professionals calibrate their practices to common standards. The work of alignment melds with the practices of collaborative inquiry when student assessments are connected to important curricular outcomes and feedback loops are developed for linking instructional practices to that curriculum.

TECHNICAL CAPACITIES

This arena names the major learning agendas for many professionals and organizations in this era of transitions. These technical knowledge and skill sets also require shifts in habits, and in some cases, shifts in formal working agreements.

ASSESSMENT LITERACY. Assessment literacy begins with having a clear purpose in mind for a given assessment and not trying to contort an available assessment to serve purposes for which it is not designed (Stiggins, 1995). Paper and pencil tests serve one set of purposes. More complex performance assessments serve another. Qualitative measures such as well-designed rubrics help students and teachers assess products and performances against a set of criteria. Criterion-based and norm-referenced measures serve distinctly different intentions.

Student assessment information is the organizing resource for the types of collaborative inquiry we explore in this volume. One practical outcome of shared inquiry in schools has been to motivate teacher work on the types of assessments they apply in their classrooms.

DATA ANALYSIS SKILLS. These abilities are both personal and collective. Pattern seeking in charts and graphs are learnable skills for individuals and groups. The tools and strategies in this book are intended to support skill development. Data analysis is organized by questions. The questions, and continuous collaborative questioning are at the heart of collaborative improvement efforts. The question-driven Collaborative Learning Cycle presented earlier in Chapter Three offers a structure for guiding and organizing data explorations.

LEARNING-FOCUSED INSTRUCTION. As described earlier, the transition from teaching-focused to learning-focused instruction is underway in many quarters. Learning-focused instruction places learners and their needs at the center of the equation. The intention of this approach is to bring learners to important content and not content to disinterested recipients. For many practitioners this shift requires an expanded repertoire and expanded ways of thinking about learning and instruction. (Saphier and Gower, 1997; Lipton and Wellman, 2000; Tomlinson 2001). Collaborative analysis of student work and assessment results focuses the conversation on learning, not teaching. This approach is psychologically safer and ultimately more effective for producing improvement in student learning. This focus stands in contrast to one that espouses some set of best practices within a specific content domain, often implying a deficiency in current practices. When teachers engage in exploration of learning results, they can make their own determinations regarding the effectiveness of present teaching practices and identify areas for expanding their skill and knowledge bases.

LEARNING-FOCUSED SUPERVISION. As teachers and schools make the transition from teaching-focused to learning-focused instruction, supervisory patterns must shift accordingly. From a systems perspective, feedback loops matter. If the feedback is about teaching, which many current systems promote, then it is quite possible for that feedback to be divorced from a focus on what is going on in the class for learners. Focusing observations and comments on classroom management, bulletin boards and the number of students who respond to teacher questions misses the point and purpose of those activities. The core purpose of supervision should be "working-on-the work" (Schlechty, 2001). In many cases this means focusing supervisory interactions on student products and performances in both the teachers' planning phases and in the teachers' reflecting phases, by exploring the meaning that teachers individually and collectively are making from their ideas, observations and analyses. This practice requires supervisory abilities for navigating back and forth across a continuum of interaction—from a coaching stance to a collaborative stance to a consultative stance during these engagements (Lipton and Wellman, 2003).

LEARNING-FOCUSED PROFESSIONAL DEVELOPMENT. With student learning results at the center of the conversation, conceptions of professional development shift from seat time rewards for enduring seminars and workshops to more focused and often school-based forms of adult learning that are driven by measurable and measured student learning needs. Gaps in student performance ultimately link to gaps in teacher knowledge and skill.

Many forms of professional development are emerging that help teachers link their own learning to student learning (Lipton and Wellman, 2001). These include practitioner networks within and between schools in which groups of educators with common interests share resources and explore new ideas in such areas as student writing, integrating technology or developing students' thinking skills. Study groups within schools and districts are another effective form of collaborative learning. Such groups often use a central book or set of articles to organize their investigation of a theme. Case studies that emerge from a particular teacher's work can also focus and engage group learning. Online resources will continue to make these types of networking possible. Web-based resources open doors to research, model programs and to other teachers. Data-driven dialogue and the tools of collaborative inquiry are especially powerful forms of professional learning.

STANDARDS-BASED GRADING AND REPORTING. With the shift to learning-focused instruction organized by clear and agreed upon standards comes the necessary reconsideration of grading and reporting systems. "What is a grade?" is an important and difficult to discuss question for teachers' conversations. Norms of privacy and autonomy create moats around personal and often highly subjective grading systems. Without agreed upon criteria and specific standards for calibration, a particular teacher's 'A' may not necessarily be the team, department or school's 'A'.

Grading issues are often a reflection of professional values and beliefs. As standards-driven student performance data becomes readily available, important and at times discomforting conversations need to be structured to sort out deeply rooted individual grading perspectives. These conversations will produce criteria grading standards at all levels of the system and, ultimately, greater degrees of inter-rater reliability.

PROFESSIONAL CAPACITIES

The structural and technical capacities described above emerge within an organizational framework. Teachers operate within the organization and within the system by applying their own professional expertise within the learning process for students. Four major capacities frame and define expertise in teaching.

KNOWLEDGE OF THE STRUCTURE OF THE CONTENT DISCIPLINE(S). Teacher knowledge of the structure of a given content discipline correlates highly with student success in that area. These understandings move beyond content knowledge alone and into the organization of that knowledge within specific content domains. The structure of the discipline means knowing the big ideas within a content area—the organizing principles, key concepts and the ways in which these concepts influence one another (Shulman, 1987). In elementary mathematics, for example, understanding means being able to explain and illustrate a sense of number and how various operations such as addition and subtraction relate to each other. In social studies it means showing students how to apply geographic, political, historical, economic and social perspectives to a given situation.

These deeper understandings greatly influence lesson design, lesson flexibility and methods for assessing learning. Teachers with rich conceptual frameworks support students in developing meaningful cognitive maps of their own (Darling-Hammond, 1997). When teachers have fragmented understandings themselves, they transfer these to their students and contribute to student misconceptions.

KNOWLEDGE OF SELF. Knowledge of self includes the territories of conceptual, ego and moral reasoning that influence the classroom environment that each teacher creates. Beliefs and values shape the perceptions and judgments that carry teachers through their days. They undergird the goals teachers set for themselves and for their students. Beliefs and values are the most influential element in the type of classroom culture and learning environment that teachers develop with their students (Pajares, 1992). High levels of moral reasoning inspire more democratic classroom practices, including teacher-to-student relationships, discipline practices and the overall emotional environment (Chang, 1994).

Knowledge of self also includes awareness of personal values, beliefs and standards that guide daily decision-making. Beliefs about the nature of learning and the purposes and processes of teaching shape curricular and instructional preferences. These beliefs also shape personal standards for what students should learn and the desired qualities of student performances and products. Further, if teachers are to be effective with an increasingly diverse student population, they need to recognize and understand their own worldview before they can appreciate and honor the worldviews of their students (McAllister and Irvine, 2000).

KNOWLEDGE OF TEACHING SKILLS AND STRATEGIES. Expert teachers, like concert violinists, consciously develop their performance repertoires. They assemble and hone micro routines that they combine and apply to fit a wide variety of conditions and settings. Master teachers automatize many routines and basic moves to free cognitive space for more sophisticated sensing of the needs of their students. Such unconscious competence is the mark of an expert in the classroom.

Content specific pedagogy is an important variable that increases student success (Wenglinsky, 2000). Students whose teachers help them to develop higher-order thinking and problem-solving skills linked to specific content areas outperform students whose teachers convey only lower order skills.

KNOWLEDGE OF LEARNERS AND LEARNING. Knowledge of who learners are and how each student learns best guides the special relationship between teacher and student. The greatest teaching repertoire in the world is wasted if it is not well matched to the needs of learners (Saphier and Gower, 1997). The push for smaller class sizes and smaller schools is a response to the need to know one another. In an increasingly diverse world, personal knowledge and close relationships help connect learners to teachers, important ideas and to each other.

The exploding knowledge base about brain development, learning styles, multiple intelligence, developmental differences and cultural patterns energizes Lee Shulman's conception of the need for pedagogical learner knowledge on the part of all teachers (Shulman, 1987). Development differences extend far beyond the primary grades. Over the years, these differences amplify as the span between students widens in Piagetian terms. There are many middle school and high school students who operate at a solid concrete operational level. These learners often bump headlong into a curriculum organized by abstractions introduced through symbol systems. When teachers recognize these learning patterns and approach instruction flexibly, they begin lessons and units with concrete experiences and then help students represent ideas with pictures and graphics. This approach supports language development and meaning making by students.

SOCIOLOGICAL INFRASTRUCTURE: HOW AND WHY WE TALK

Three focus areas shape productive school and organizational cultures: attention to task, attention to process and attention to relationship.

ATTENTION TO TASK. A group's task focus is ultimately its greatest statement of values. High performing groups develop task priorities that are congruent with their values and connected to larger systems issues. To be time and energy efficient, productive groups establish and maintain clear agendas, clear timeframes, and clear task and product success criteria. Effective data use is a central element to all of these attributes of task success.

ATTENTION TO PROCESS. Task success hinges on the process toolkit that groups develop and hone for themselves. Shared tools and structures promote successful task completion and group development. Templates and tools provide process guidance and degrees of emotional safety when groups need to address difficult topics and difficult conversations. These frameworks and structures provide navigational aides and thinking supports to help groups and group members refocus if they deviate from task agreements and procedural guidelines.

ATTENTION TO RELATIONSHIP. Task focus, process skills development and group member relationships form a synergistic whole. Each leg of this triangle supports and enhances the others. Continuous improvement requires that groups develop and monitor shared norms. They use these norms to filter choices, decisions and choice-making and decision-making processes.

Inside collaborative teaching cultures, members consciously balance participation by seeking and honoring the perspectives of others. An appreciation for the contributions of productive conflict in the group helps individuals and the group as a whole shape and reshape perspectives and proposals.

Shared focus on and shared responsibility for student learning emerges within professional communities that draw on data to assess and reflect upon practice. Within such professional relationships group members actively question and explore individual and collective teaching practices, calibrating them against clear and agreed upon standards.

LEARNING TO LEARN

The structures and capacities for school improvement outlined in this chapter and illustrated in Figure 6.1 are the ongoing work of professionals in schools. As we continue to learn more about learners and learning, we will all continue to expand and refine skills within each of these arenas. Schools will need to manage these learning agendas at multiple levels: helping students learn and learn to learn; helping professionals learn and learn to learn; and helping the organization learn and learn to learn.

"*Life is about creation. . . . A living system produces itself; it will change in order to preserve that self. Change is prompted only when an organism decides that changing is the only way to maintain itself.*"

—*Margaret J. Wheatley*

Notes

Annual Review: Ups and Downs

1. **On your own, think of three high points related to _____.**

   Write each high point on the same color sticky note; one idea per note. Label your sticky notes.

2. **On your own, think of three low points related to _____.**

   Write each high point on the second color sticky note; one idea per note. Label your sticky notes.

3. **On the wall grid, post your high points above the line, rating them by degree (+1, +2). Do the same with your low points (–1, –2)**

4. **With your table group, review the wall graph. Be ready to share your observations, insights and questions.**

See Ch. 5: pg. 76

Annual Review: Ups and Downs

Mediative Questions

1. **How does the display compare to what you would have expected it to look like?**

2. **What are some patterns you're noticing regarding the display?**

3. **What are some surprises for you?**

4. **How might you compare highs and lows?**

5. **What are some generalizations you might make?**

Artifact Hunt

1. With your table group, collect and/or envision artifacts you might show to a visitor from another culture as a means of explaining what is important to your school or organization. These might be examples of events, rituals, routines or objects that have meaning for the group.

2. Categorize your collections and make a list of your categories on the chart paper.

3. Beneath each category, record the values and beliefs represented by the artifacts within that category. NOTE: There are likely to be both positive and negative values.

4. Select an artifact or artifacts that exemplify important values within the existing state of the culture. Be ready to share your items (and thinking) with the larger group.

5. Identify and select 3-4 core values within the culture you will need to address in order to successfully implement the change initiative. Again, note that these core values may have a positive or negative effect on the plan.

6. Imagine a specific date in the future when we might "revisit" this culture as anthropologists. List artifacts, events, rituals and routines we might find as evidence of successful implementation of our change initiative.

Assumptions Card Stack and Shuffle

1. **Individually: Create a stack of cards that hold some of your assumptions* about: _____.**

2. **Placing all cards in the center of the table: Stack and Shuffle.**

3. **In turn, each group member picks a card to read aloud to the table group. Members engage in dialogue and discussion about the items.**

*one assumption per card

Assumptions Card Stack and Shuffle

Mediating Questions:

- What is the thinking behind this assumption?

- What are some inferences that can be made from it?

- What might be some alternative interpretations?

- To what degree is this assumption generalizable or context specific?

- If _____ were true, would this assumption still hold?

Consensogram Guiding Questions

- **What are some of your predictions and assumptions?**

- **What are some of the things you are noticing about the data on the graphs?**

- **What important points seem to "pop-out"?**

- **What are some patterns, categories or trends that are emerging?**

- **What seems to be surprising or unexpected?**

- **What are some things we have not yet explored?**

- **What inferences/explanations/conclusions might we draw?**

Creating Rubrics

Topic: _____

Primary Trait			
	Burlap	Corduroy	Velvet

First Turn/Last Turn

1. **Read individually. Highlight 2–3 items.**

2. **In turn share one of your items but do not comment on it.**

3. **Group members comment—in round-robin fashion*—about the item (without cross-talk).**

4. **The initial person who named the item then shares his or her thinking about the item and takes the last turn, making the final comments.**

5. **Repeat the pattern around the table.**

* Round-robin is a highly structured participation strategy. Group members speak in turns, moving around the table in one direction.

Fishbone Diagram

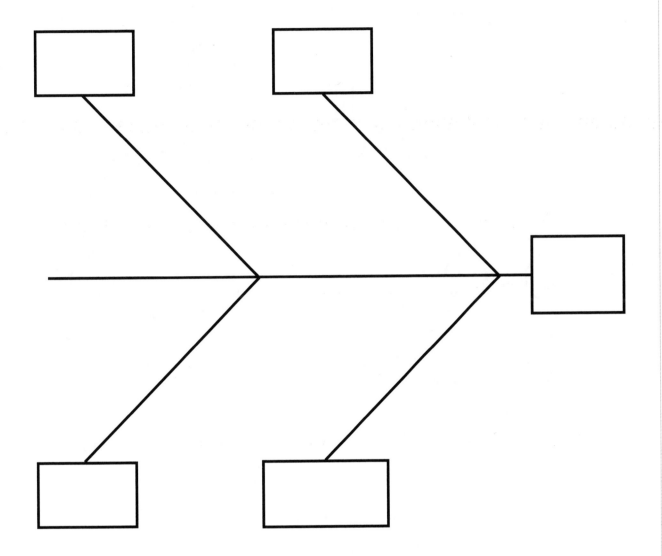

Futures Wheel

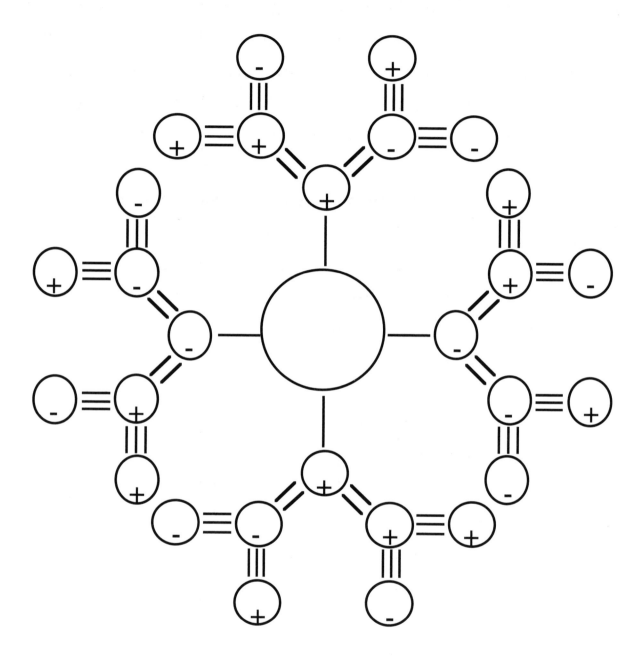

See Ch. 5: pg. 96   www.miravia.com MiraVia, LLC • 3 Lost Acre Trail • Sherman CT 06784 860.354.4543

HERE'S WHAT!	SO WHAT?	NOW WHAT?

Idea, Category and Web

1. **Prepare a T-chart. Label the columns idea and category.**

2. **Place the topic for idea and category generation on the top of the chart paper.**

3. **One group member offers an idea and records it in the idea column.**

4. **The idea generator, or another group member, proposes a category within which the idea fits and records it in the category column.**

   Note: Each category may be used only once. The goal is to generate broad categories for elaboration during the webbing phase.

5. **Continue the process. Develop 6–12 idea/category pairs.**

6. **On a large piece of chart paper draw a web diagram with the topic in the center and each category in a separate circle branching out from the center.**

7. **Once all of the category labels are transferred, add details to the web, category by category.**

See Ch. 5: pg. 100   www.miravia.com MiraVia, LLC • 3 Lost Acre Trail • Sherman CT 06784 860.354.4543

Interrelationship Diagram

1. Select a problem, process or system to explore.

2. Brainstorm a list of the major categories of issues related to the selected topic. Tip: Hold the number of categories to 6-8. More than this can be difficult to manage.

3. Arrange the names of the major categories randomly in a circle around a sheet of chart paper. You can do this directly on the chart paper or use sticky notes that can be rearranged if needed during the drafting process.

4. Select one category as a starting point. Ask two-way questions to determine whether this category is a driver or an effect of the each of the other categories. Draw arrows from the drivers to the effects. Continue in this way through each of the categories. Caution: There can never be two-headed arrows. The group must decide which category dominates the other.

5. Count the number of arrows going away from each category. Rank the drivers from highest to lowest in impact.

6. Count the number of arrows pointing towards each category. Rank the effects from highest to lowest in terms of major outcomes of the current problem, process or system.

7. Study the results and select intervention points that amplify desired results and minimize less desirable outcomes.

Interrelationship Diagram

Topic: _____

Drivers   **Effects**

See Ch. 5: pg. 102   www.miravia.com MiraVia, LLC • 3 Lost Acre Trail • Sherman CT 06784 860.354.4543

Interrelationship Diagram

Student Mathematics Achievement

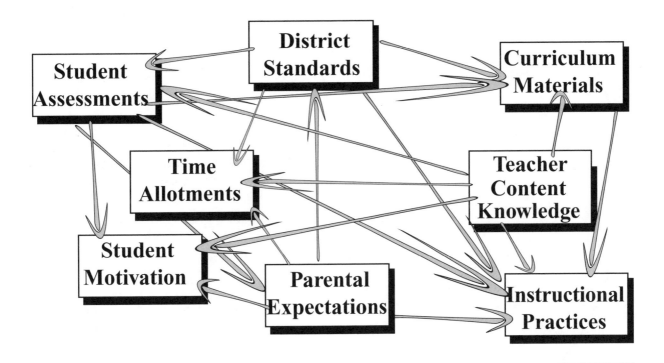

Drivers
- District Standards
- Teacher content knowledge
- Parental expectations
- Student assessments

Effects
- Instructional Practices
- Time allotments
- Student motivation
- Curriculum materials

See Ch. 5: pg. 102

Inter-VENN-tion

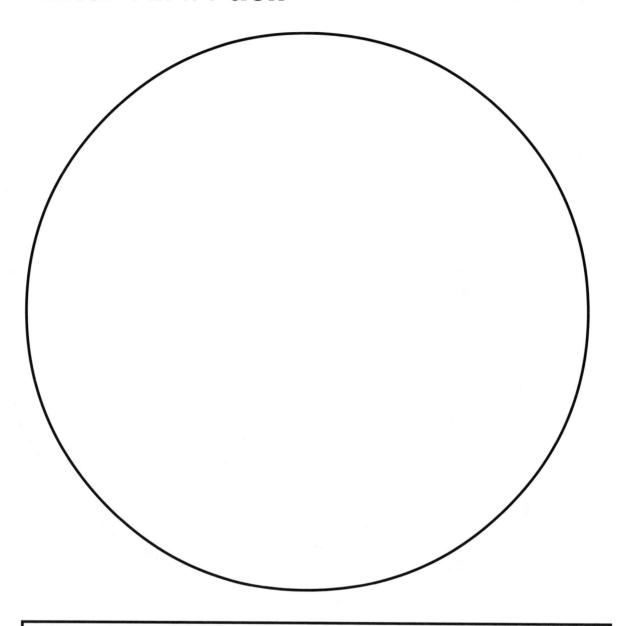

My learning goal . . .

See Ch. 5: pg. 104   www.miravia.com MiraVia, LLC • 3 Lost Acre Trail • Sherman CT 06784 860.354.4543

Inter-VENN-tion

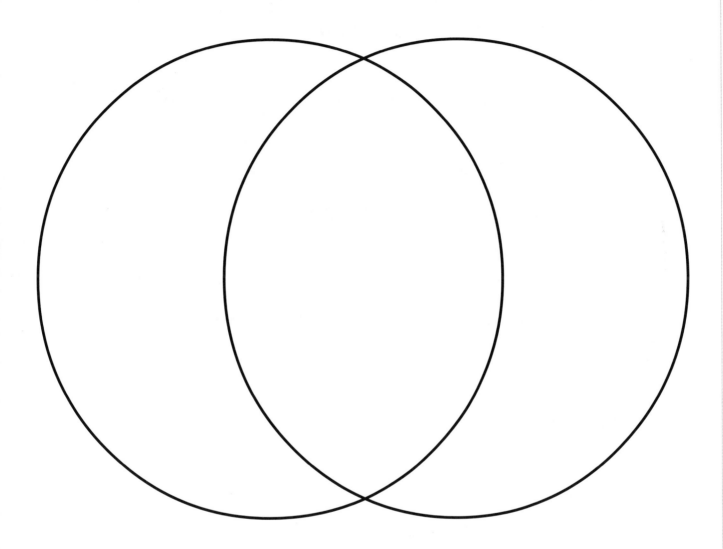

Share your learning goals here:

Round the Room and Back Again

1. On a sheet of paper write one example of the topic the group is about to explore.

2. Set aside your writing materials. At the signal, move around the room sharing your examples and listening to the examples of others. The challenge is to rely only on auditory memory.

3. At the second signal, return to your seat and recording materials and write down as many examples as you can recall.

4. Pool your examples with your table group, and extend your list.

Say Something

1. **Choose a partner.**

2. **Read silently to the designated stopping point.**

3. **When each partner is ready, stop and "say something"***

4. **Continue the process until you have completed the selection.**

   * 'something' might be a question, a brief summary, a key point, an interesting idea or personal connection.

Synectics—Four Box

_____ **is**

like a(n) _____

because . . .

See Ch. 5: pg. 112   www.miravia.com MiraVia, LLC • 3 Lost Acre Trail • Sherman CT 06784 860.354.4543

Walk-Around Survey

1. **Individual Work.** On your own, generate a response for each category in the left-hand column of the page.

2. **Full-Group Exchange.** With your survey form, walk around the room filling your form by surveying group members for their responses. Briefly capture your colleagues' thinking, as well as their names, in each appropriate box. Don't collect information from your own table group; you will have an opportunity to exchange thinking with them later on.

3. **Table-Group Processing.** Return to your table group and share your collected information, as well as your own thinking.

4. **Table-Group Analysis.** As you pool and share your data, analyze the information you have collected; look for themes, compare and contrast the items, organize into new categories.

5. **Generating Theory:** Identify a pattern or theme in the data from which you can develop a hypothesis or generate a theory about the group. Be ready to share your theory, with connections to the supporting data, using a What and Why reporting pattern. [What: your theory/Why: some of your supporting data].

Walk-Around Survey

Topic: _____

See Ch. 5: pg. 114   www.miravia.com MiraVia, LLC • 3 Lost Acre Trail • Sherman CT 06784 860.354.4543

Meeting Partners

Make an appointment with 4 different people—one for each image. Be sure you each record the appointment on your page, by writing your partner's name in the available space. Only make the appointment if there is an open slot at that spot on each of your forms.

_____

_____

_____

Notes

Appendix

This section provides a selection of resources to enhance and supplement the materials in this volume. Included in this Appendix you will find:

APPENDIX A: ASSESSMENT: A GLOSSARY OF USEFUL TERMS

This section offers a list of frequently used terms and their definitions related to assessment. The glossary is intended to support group work by establishing clear definitions and common understanding.

APPENDIX B: GROUP DEVELOPMENT RUBRIC

This rubric supports groups in assessing their development in three domains: attention to task; attention to process; and attention to relationship. Each domain has a three level scale ranging from *unaware* to *with conscious competence* to *flexibly and fluently.*

APPENDIX C: STRATEGY STACKS

Jumpstart your planning with these samples of strategies that can be stacked to engage participants in productive, learning-focused meetings. The tools can be sequenced to construct meetings of various lengths, while applying the principles of the Collaborative Learning Cycle and supporting the cognitive and affective intentions related to each phase.

APPENDIX D: TEN STRATEGIES FOR GETTING STARTED

These ten strategies are quick starters for meetings and work sessions. Each strategy activates prior knowledge and supports community building among group members, and works flexibly with any topic. Several of these strategies can also be used to organize and integrate learning for participants at the ending of a session.

APPENDIX E: TYPES OF SURVEY OR INTERVIEW QUESTIONS

This section presents a selection of survey and interview questions for use in assessment tool design. These examples illustrate a variety of question types and purposes and can also be used directly as a resource bank for developing surveys and formal and informal interview questionnaires.

APPENDIX F: EQUIPMENT MATERIALS LIST

This equipment list can be used as is or as a model for designing your own version. Checklists organize and clarify communication and make session planning more time and energy efficient. This is particularly so when sessions are spaced apart in time and details are hard to remember.

APPENDIX G: THINKING ABOUT ROOM DESIGN

This room design schematic presents a model of one way to set up a large meeting room. The table arrangement facilitates small group interaction and provides clear sightlines to projected images and central information displays.

APPENDIX A—Assessment: A Glossary of Useful Terms

The following is a list of frequently used terms related to assessment practices. This glossary is intended to support group work by establishing clear definitions and common understanding.

ACCOUNTABILITY. The demand by a community, e.g., public officials, employers and taxpayers, for school officials to demonstrate that resources invested in education have led to measurable learning. Accountability testing is an attempt to sample what students have learned, or how well teachers have taught, and/or the effectiveness of a school principal's performance as an instructional leader. School budgets and personnel promotions, compensation, and awards may be affected by the degree to which a school or district demonstrates effectiveness. Most states and provinces require that these assessment results be made public.

Accountability is often viewed as an important factor in education reform. An assessment system connected to accountability helps identify the needs of schools so that resources can be equitably distributed. In this context, accountability measures include such indicators as equity, competency of teaching staff, physical infrastructure, curriculum, class size, instructional methods, existence of tracking, number of higher cost students, dropout rates, and parental involvement as well as student test scores. An underlying assumption of these requirements is that test scores analyzed in a disaggregated format help identify instructional problems and point to potential solutions.

ACHIEVEMENT TEST. A standardized test designed to efficiently measure the amount of knowledge and/or skill a learner has acquired, usually as a result of classroom instruction. Such test results are organized as a statistical profile and used as a measurement to evaluate student learning in comparison with a standard or norm.

ACTION RESEARCH. District, school and classroom-based studies initiated and conducted by teachers and other school staff. This process involves teachers, aides, principals, and other school staff as researchers who systematically reflect on their teaching or other work, generate questions or hypotheses and collect data that will inform their practice. It offers staff an opportunity to explore issues of interest to them in an effort to improve classroom instruction and educational effectiveness.

AFFECTIVE. Outcomes of education that involve feelings more than cognition, e.g., emotional responses and social skills.

ALTERNATIVE ASSESSMENT. These assessments complement or replace traditional, standardized, norm- or criterion-referenced paper and pencil testing. Students might be required to answer an open-ended question, work out a solution to a problem, perform a demonstration of a skill, or in

www.miravia.com MiraVia, LLC • 3 Lost Acre Trail • Sherman CT 06784 860.354.4543

some way produce work rather than select an answer from choices on a sheet of paper. Portfolios and instructor observation of students are also alternative forms of assessment.

APTITUDE TEST. A test intended to measure the test-taker's innate ability to learn, usually given before receiving instruction.

ASSESSMENT. The Latin root *assidere* means to sit beside. In an educational context, the process of observing learning; describing, collecting, recording, scoring, and interpreting information about a student's or one's own learning. At its most useful, assessment is an episode in the learning process; part of reflection and autobiographical understanding of progress. Traditionally, student assessments are used to determine placement, promotion, graduation, or retention.

In the context of institutional accountability, assessments are undertaken to determine the effectiveness of schools and school personnel. In the context of school improvement, assessment is an essential tool for evaluating the effectiveness of changes in the teaching-learning process.

ASSESSMENT LITERACY. The possession of knowledge about the basic principles of sound assessment practice, including terminology, the development and use of assessment methodologies and techniques, familiarity with standards of quality in assessment and increasingly, familiarity with alternatives to traditional measurements of learning.

ASSESSMENT TASK. An illustrative task or performance opportunity that closely targets defined instructional aims, allowing students to demonstrate their progress and capabilities.

AUTHENTIC ASSESSMENT. Evaluating by asking for the behavior the learning is intended to produce within a relevant context. The concept of model, practice, feedback in which students know what excellent performance is and are guided to practice an entire concept rather than bits and pieces in preparation for eventual understanding. A variety of techniques can be employed in authentic assessment.

The goal of authentic assessment is to gather evidence that students can use knowledge effectively and be able to critique their own efforts. Authentic assessment implies that evaluating progress should be a central experience in the learning process and is conducted at regular intervals. Patterns of success and failure are observed by an assessor as learners apply their knowledge and skills to purposeful problems and tasks (see *Learning-Embedded Assessment*).

BENCHMARK. (1) An actual measurement of group performance against an established standard at defined points along the path toward the standard. Subsequent measurements of group performance use the benchmarks to measure progress toward achievement. (2) Examples of student achievement that illustrate points on a performance scale, used as exemplars.

COHORT. A defined group whose progress is followed by means of measurements at different points in time. For example, tracking a cohort in Math would include reviewing standardized test scores for 4th graders in 2001 and for the same students as 6th graders in 2003.

COMPETENCY TEST. A test intended to establish that a student has met established minimum standards of skills and knowledge and is thus eligible for promotion, graduation, certification, or other official acknowledgement of achievement.

CRITERION REFERENCED TESTS. A test in which performance is compared to an expected level of mastery in a content area rather than to other students' scores. Such tests usually include questions based on what the student was taught and are designed to measure the student's mastery of designated objectives of an instructional program. The *criterion* is the standard of performance established as the passing score for the test. Criterion referenced tests can have norms, but comparison to a norm is not the purpose of the assessment.

Criterion referenced tests have also been used to provide information for program evaluation, especially to track the success or progress of schools and student populations that have been involved in change or that are at risk of inequity. In this case, the tests are not used to compare teachers, teams or buildings within a district but rather to give feedback on progress of groups and individuals.

CURRICULUM-EMBEDDED OR LEARNING-EMBEDDED ASSESSMENT. Assessment that occurs concurrently with instructional processes such as projects, portfolios and exhibitions. Tasks or tests are developed from the curriculum or instructional materials and are conducted within the classroom setting.

CUT SCORE. Score used to determine the minimum performance level needed to pass a competency test (see *Descriptor* for another type of determinor).

DESCRIPTOR. A set of signs used as a scale against which a performance or product is placed in an evaluation. For example, to achieve a 5 out of a possible 6 on a writing test, "The student describes the problem adequately and argues convincingly for at least one solution." Descriptors allow assessments to include clear guidelines for what is and is not valued in student work.

DIMENSION. Aspects or categories in which performance in a domain or subject area will be judged. Separate descriptors or scoring methods may apply to each dimension of the student's performance assessment.

ESSAY TEST. A test that requires students to answer questions in writing. Responses can be brief or extensive. Tests for recall and ability to apply knowledge of a subject to questions about the subject.

EVALUATION. Both qualitative and quantitative descriptions of student behavior plus value judgments concerning the desirability of that behavior. Using collected information (assessments) to make informed decisions about continued instruction, programs, activities.

GRADE EQUIVALENT. A score that describes student performance in terms of the statistical performance of an average student at a given grade level. A grade equivalent score of 5.5, for example, might indicate that the student's score is what could be expected of an average student doing average work in the fifth month of the fifth grade. This score allows for a theoretical or approximate comparison across grades. It ranges from September of the kindergarten year (K.O.) to June of the senior year in high school (12.9) Useful as a ranking score, grade equivalents are only a theoretical or approximate comparison across grades and may not indicate what the student would actually score on a test.

FORMATIVE ASSESSMENT. In process observations and measurements designed to determine the degree to which students know or are able to do a given learning task, as well as what they are not yet able to do. Used to suggest future steps for teaching and learning (see *Summative Assessment*).

HIGH STAKES TESTING. Any testing program whose results have important consequences for students, teachers, schools, and/or districts. Such stakes may include promotion, certification, graduation, or denial/ approval of services and opportunity.

HOLISTIC SCORING METHOD. This method of assessment assigns a single score based on an overall assessment of performance rather than scoring or analyzing dimensions individually. The quality of a final product or performance is evaluated rather than individual elements. A holistic scoring rubric might combine a number of elements on a single scale.

ITEM ANALYSIS. Analyzing each item on a test to determine the proportions of students selecting each answer. Can be used to evaluate strengths and weaknesses of individual or groups of students, or to explore problems with the test's validity or possible bias.

JOURNALS, Journals are students' personal records and reactions to various aspects of their learning, often as responses to specific prompts.

MEAN. One of several ways of representing a group with a single, typical score. It is figured by adding up all the individual scores in a group and dividing them by the number of people in the group. Can be affected by extremely low or high scores.

MEASUREMENT. Quantitative description of student learning and/or qualitative description of student dispositions.

MEDIAN. The point on a scale that divides a group into two equal subgroups. Another way to represent a group's scores with a single, typical score. The median is not affected by low or high scores as is the mean (see *Norm*).

METACOGNITION. The knowledge of one's own thinking processes and strategies, and the ability to consciously reflect and act on the knowledge of cognition to modify those processes and strategies.

MULTIDIMENSIONAL ASSESSMENT. Assessment that gathers information about a broad spectrum of abilities and skills (as in Howard Gardner's theory of Multiple Intelligences).

MULTIPLE CHOICE TESTS. A test in which students are presented with a question or an incomplete sentence or idea. The students are expected to choose the correct or best answer/completion from a menu of alternatives.

NORM. A distribution of scores obtained from a norm group. The norm is the midpoint (or median) of scores or performance of the students in that group. Fifty percent will score above and fifty percent below the norm.

NORM GROUP. A random group of students selected by a test developer to take a test providing a range of scores and determining the percentiles of performance for use in establishing scoring standards.

NORM REFERENCED TESTS. A test in which a student or a group's performance is compared to that of a norm group. The student or group scores will not fall evenly on either side of the median established by the original test takers. The results are relative to the performance of an external group and are designed to be compared with the norm group providing a performance standard. Often used to measure and compare students, schools, districts, and states on the basis of norm-established scales of achievement.

NORMAL CURVE EQUIVALENT (NCE). A score that ranges from 1–99, often used by testers to manipulate data arithmetically. Used to compare different tests for the same student or group of students and between different students on the same test. An NCE is a normalized test score with a mean of 50 and a standard deviation of 21.06. NCEs should be used instead of percentiles for comparative purposes. Required by many categorical funding agencies, e.g., Chapter I or Title I.

OBJECTIVE TEST. A test for which the scoring procedure is completely specified enabling agreement among different scorers, or inter-rater reliability. The test items have only one correct answer.

www.miravia.com MiraVia, LLC • 3 Lost Acre Trail • Sherman CT 06784 860.354.4543

ON-DEMAND ASSESSMENT. A decontextualized assessment process taking place as a scheduled event outside the normal routine. An attempt to summarize what students have learned that is not embedded in classroom activity.

OUTCOME. An operationally defined educational goal, usually a culminating activity, product, or performance that can be measured.

PERCENTILE. A ranking scale ranging from a low of 1 to a high of 99 with 50 as the median score. A percentile rank indicates the percentage of a reference or norm group obtaining scores equal to or less than the test-taker's score. A percentile score does not refer to the percentage of questions answered correctly, it indicates the test-taker's standing relative to the norm group standard.

PERFORMANCE-BASED ASSESSMENT. Direct, systematic observation and rating of student performance of an educational objective, often an ongoing observation over a period of time, and typically involving the creation of products. The assessment may be a continuing interaction between teacher and student and should ideally be part of the learning process. The assessment should be a real-world performance with relevance to the student and learning community. Assessment of the performance is done using a rubric, or analytic scoring guide to aid in objectivity.

PERFORMANCE CRITERIA. The standards by which student performance is evaluated. Performance criteria help assessors maintain objectivity and provide students with important information about expectations, giving them a target or goal for which to strive.

PORTFOLIO. A systematic and organized collection of a student's work that exhibits the direct evidence of a student's efforts, achievements, and progress over a period of time. Ideally, the collection should involve the student in selection of its contents, and should include information about the performance criteria, the rubric or criteria for judging merit, and evidence of student self-reflection or evaluation. It should include representative work, providing a documentation of the learner's performance and a basis for evaluation of the student's progress. Portfolios may include a variety of demonstrations of learning and have been gathered in the form of a physical collection of materials, videos, CD-ROMs, reflective journals, etc.

PORTFOLIO ASSESSMENT. Use of a collection of student work, or portfolio, to determine degree of learning. Portfolios may be assessed in a variety of ways. The portfolio might be assessed for the presence of required pieces, or each item may be individually scored, or a holistic scoring process might be used and an evaluation made on the basis of an overall impression of the student's collected work. It is common that assessors work together to establish consensus of standards or to ensure greater reliability in evaluation of student work. Established criteria, rubrics and exemplars are often used by reviewers and students involved in the process of evaluating progress and achievement of objectives.

PRIMARY TRAIT METHOD. A type of scoring constructed to assess a specific trait, skill, behavior, or format, or the evaluation of the primary impact of a learning process on a designated audience.

PRIMARY TRAIT RUBRIC. Sometimes called analytic scoring rubric, this type of rubric scoring separates the whole into categories of criteria that are examined one at a time. Student writing, for example, might be scored on the basis of grammar, organization, and clarity of ideas. Useful as a diagnostic tool, an analytic scale is effective when there are several dimensions on which the piece of work will be evaluated (see Rubric).

PROCESS. A generalizable method of doing something, most often involving steps or operations which are usually ordered and/or interdependent. Process can be evaluated as part of an assessment, for example, evaluating a student's performance during pre-writing exercises leading up to the final production of an essay or paper.

PRODUCT. The tangible and stable result of a performance or task. Student performance can be evaluated based on a product designed to demonstrate degree of learning.

PROFILE. A graphic compilation of the performance of an individual on a series of assessments.

PROJECT. A complex assignment involving more than one type of activity and production. Projects can take a variety of forms, some examples are a mural construction, a shared service project, or other collaborative or individual effort.

QUALITATIVE DATA. Non-numerical data, often in the form of categorical data or non-quantified narrative information. A record of thoughts, observations, opinions, or words. Qualitative data typically comes from asking open-ended questions to which the answers are not limited by a set of choices or a scale. These data are descriptive in nature. Answers questions about how and why. Examples include information gathered from focus groups, in-depth interviews and case studies; generally examines attitudes, feelings and motivations. While these data can be categorized in some way, they generally cannot be reduced to numerical measurements.

QUANTITATIVE DATA. Information presented in the form of numbers, percentages or statistics—for example, a 15% improvement in a child's reading level as measured by a reading pre-test and post-test. Quantitative data answers in numerical terms such questions as "how often" and "how many," and is used for correlational studies (i.e., a comparison of different programs, geographic locations, or time periods), and for tracking change over time (i.e., changes in rates of coverage, or percentage of the target population reached).

QUARTILE. The breakdown of an aggregate of percentile rankings into four categories: the 0–25th percentile, 26–50th percentile, etc.

QUINTILE. The breakdown of an aggregate of percentile rankings into five categories: the 0–20th percentile, 21–40th percentile, etc.

RATING SCALE. A scale based on descriptive words or phrases that indicate performance levels. Qualities of a performance are described (e.g., advanced, intermediate, novice) in order to designate a level of achievement. These scales are often used with rubrics.

RELIABILITY. The measure of consistency for an assessment instrument. The instrument should yield similar results over time with similar populations in similar circumstances.

RUBRIC. A rubric is a scoring guide used in subjective assessments. A rubric implies that a rule defining the criteria of an assessment system is followed in evaluation. A rubric can be an explicit description of performance characteristics corresponding to a point on a rating scale. A scoring rubric makes explicit expected qualities of performance on a rating scale or the definition of a single scoring point on a scale (see *holistic* and *primary trait rubric*).

SAMPLING. (1) A way to obtain information about a large group by examining a smaller, randomly chosen selection (the sample) of group members. The results are expected to be representative of the group as a whole. (2) Sampling may also refer to the choice of smaller tasks or processes that will be valid for making inferences about the student's performance in a larger domain. "Matrix sampling" asks different groups to take small segments of a test; the results reflect the ability of the larger group on a complete range of tasks.

SCALE. A classification tool or counting system designed to indicate and measure the degree to which an event or behavior has occurred.

SCALE SCORES. Scores based on a scale ranging from 001 to 999. Scale scores are useful in comparing performance in one subject area across classes, schools, districts, and other large populations, especially in monitoring change over time.

SCORE. A rating of performance based on a scale or classification.

SCORING. A package of guidelines intended for people scoring performance assessments. May include instructions for raters, notes on training raters, rating scales and samples of student work exemplifying various levels of performance.

SCORING CRITERIA. Rules for assigning a score or the dimensions of proficiency in performance used to describe a student's response to a task. May include rating scales, checklists, answer keys, rubrics, and other scoring tools.

SELF-ASSESSMENT. A process in which students engage in a systematic review of their performance, critiquing their own work, usually for the purpose of improving future performance. Usually involves comparison with a standard, established criteria.

SENIOR PROJECT. Extensive projects planned and carried out during the senior year of high school as the culmination of the secondary school experience, senior projects require higher-level thinking skills, problem-solving, and creative thinking. They are often interdisciplinary, and may require extensive research. Projects culminate in a presentation of the project to a panel of people, usually faculty and community mentors, sometimes students, who evaluate the student's work at the end of the year.

STANDARDIZED TEST. An objective test that is given and scored in a uniform manner. Standardized tests are carefully constructed and items are selected after trials for appropriateness and difficulty. Tests are issued with a manual giving complete guidelines for administration and scoring. The guidelines attempt to eliminate variables that might influence test results. Scores are often norm-referenced.

STANDARDS. Agreed upon values used to measure the quality of student performance, instructional methods, curriculum, etc.

SUBJECTIVE ASSESSMENT. Assessment in which the impression or opinion of the assessor determines the score or evaluation of performance. A test in which the answers cannot be known or prescribed in advance.

SUMMATIVE ASSESSMENT. Evaluation at the conclusion of a unit or units of instruction used to determine or judge student skills and knowledge or effectiveness of a plan or activity. Also used at the conclusion of a program or plan of activity to determine the effectiveness of that program or plan.

VALIDITY. The test measures the desired performance and appropriate inferences can be drawn from the results. The assessment accurately reflects the learning it was designed to measure.

Adapted from: *An Assessment Terminology: A Glossary of Useful Terms.* New Horizons for Learning. www.newhorizons.org

APPENDIX B: *Group Development Rubric*

ATTENTION TO TASK		Unaware	Conscious Incompetence	With Conscious Competency	Flexibly and Fluently
Learning-Focused	• The group establishes task priorities that are congruent with organizational values				
	• The group uses data to focus its attention and energy				
	• The group relates specific tasks to larger systems issues and frameworks				
Time and Energy Efficient	• The group establishes and maintains clear task and product success criteria				
	• The group establishes and maintains clear task agendas				
	• The group establishes and maintains clear time frames for its work				
Data-Driven	• The group collects and selects relevant data for its work				
	• The group develops and utilizes effective data displays				
	• The group uses data effectively to make decisions				

ATTENTION TO PROCESS		Unaware	Conscious Incompetence	With Conscious Competency	Flexibly and Fluently
Shared Tools and Structures	• The group develops and applies shared tools and structures				
	• The group follows agreed upon protocols				
	• The group refocuses if members deviate from task agreements or process guidelines				
Learning-Focused Conversations	• Group members invite and sustain the thinking of others (pausing, paraphrasing, inquiring)				
	• Group members give their full attention to others (eye contact, listening nonjudgmentally, listening without interrupting)				
	• Group members balance advocacy for their own ideas with inquiry into the ideas of others				
Data-Driven Dialogue	• The group uses data to focus and calibrate conversations				
	• Group members inquire into and clarify assumptions; their own and others				
	• Group members seek shared understanding				

www.miravia.com MiraVia, LLC • 3 Lost Acre Trail • Sherman CT 06784 860.354.4543

ATTENTION TO RELATIONSHIP		Unaware	Conscious Incompetence	With Conscious Competency	Flexibly and Fluently
Shared Norms and Values	• The group develops norms that ensure psychological safety for all group members				
	• Group members behave congruently with agreed upon norms				
	• The group filters choices and decisions through agreed upon values				
Collaborative Cultures	• Group members balance participation and encourage and elicit contributions from others				
	• Group members seek and honor diverse perspectives				
	• Group members anticipate and accept that productive conflict contributes to group success				
Professional Community	• Group members actively question and explore individual and collective teaching practices and calibrate them against clear and agreed upon standards				
	• Group members engage purposely with relevant tasks that are focused on student learning				
	• Group members consistently use data to self assess and reflect				

APPENDIX C: *Strategy Stacks*

The strategies described in Chapter Five are flexible and can be applied to one or more phases in the Collaborative Learning Cycle. They are generic and can be applied to a variety of topics. This combination of qualities makes these tools effective as a strategy stack. That is, you can sequence several strategies to engage participants in productive, learning-focused meetings. The following strategy stacks are offered as examples. As you develop your meeting designs, we encourage you to draw from the Strategies for Getting Started (Appendix D), as well as strategies from your present repertoire.

45–60 MINUTE MEETING

STRATEGY STACK	TOPIC EXAMPLE: ASSESSMENT
Activating and Engaging: First Word	First Word: Assessment
Exploring and Discovering: Say Something	Research synthesis or other appropriate text
Organizing and Integrating: Here's What!/So What?/ Now What?	Here's What: A new idea you intend to try, So What: How it might influence your work, Now What: First step in getting started

60–90 MINUTE MEETING

STRATEGY STACK	TOPIC EXAMPLE: HIGH PERFORMING GROUPS
Activating and Engaging: Idea/ Category and . . .	Chart ideas and categories for high performing groups
Exploring and Discovering: Web (with Walk-about variation)	Web the Categories and Ideas from the Activating and Engaging phase
Organizing and Integrating: Matchbook Definition	Craft a definition for high performing groups

TWO TO THREE HOUR MEETING

STRATEGY STACK	TOPIC EXAMPLE: GRADING POLICY
Activating and Engaging: A–Z Listing	Generate issues related to grading
Exploring and Discovering: First Turn/ Last Turn	Research synthesis, or other appropriate text; or copy of present grading policies
Organizing and Integrating: Four-box Synectics	Grading is like (what household object) because . . .

www.miravia.com MiraVia, LLC • 3 Lost Acre Trail • Sherman CT 06784 860.354.4543

FULL-DAY MEETING

Strategy Stack	Topic Example: Reviewing Math Data
Activating and Engaging: Visual Synectics	Choose an appropriate visual: Mathematics is like (image) because . . .
Exploring and Discovering: Consensogram	See tool description for tips on developing questions
Organizing and Integrating: Color Question Brainstorming	Generate color questions about math teaching and learning
LUNCH	
Activating and Engaging: Value Voting	e.g., Rate your degree of satisfaction with this morning's work
Exploring and Discovering: Collaborative Learning Cycle	Run a full cycle, using data previously organized and ready for display
Organizing and Integrating: Agreement on theory or next steps	Generate one or more theories of causality; and/or theories of action; agree on next steps

TWO MEETING SEQUENCE

Strategy Stack: First Meeting	Topic Example: Increasing Student Engagement
Activating and Engaging: Brainstorm and Categorize	Generate and sort items that influence student engagement
Exploring and Discovering: Interrelationship Diagram	Use categories from Brainstorm and Categorize for the first stage in the diagram
Organizing and Integrating: Last Word	Last Word: Engagement

Strategy Stack: Second Meeting	Topic Example: Increasing Student Engagement
Activating and Engaging: Paired Verbal Fluency	Prompt: What you recall from our last meeting
Exploring and Discovering: Fishbone	Transfer the Drivers from the first meeting's Interrelationship Diagram to the Fishbone skeleton
Organizing and Integrating: Create A Rubric	Student engagement: low to high

APPENDIX D: *Ten Strategies for Getting Started*

What happens early in a session often establishes the tone for how group members will participate during the remainder of their time together that day. These strategies for getting groups started have the added advantage of allowing the meeting to begin on time, since they do not require that the full quorum be present.

The examples within each strategy are intended as examples only. Use these flexible structures to generate your own context specific applications.

FIRST ITEM

First Item is a round-robin pattern in which each participant in a small group has 20–30 seconds to comment in turn about something important about the first item on the agenda. This starter assumes that the first item on the agenda is the most important item for that session.

KEYWORDS*

Keywords is a round-robin pattern in which each participant offers a personal key word to start the meeting. Examples include: a word that captures how you're feeling about your day thus far; a word that captures your hopes for this session; a word that captures an impression about the last session the group had; or a word that captures a concern or experience with the topic under consideration.

IN YOUR POCKET*

Instead of offering keywords, participants select an object from their pocket, purse, or briefcase and use it as a metaphor or explanatory device to describe their day thus far; their hopes for the session; an impression of the group's last session; or a concern or expectation about the topics under consideration for the present session.

FINDING COMMON GROUND

Finding Common Ground is a table group activity for starting a session or for use after regrouping a larger group into smaller working clusters. Table groups are given a tight time frame, usually 2–3 minutes to generate 3–4 non-obvious things that they have in common. Each group is then called upon to share one of its common ground items ("We all own motorcycles"). If others in the room share that attribute, they raise their hands to indicate affiliation with the table group members who are sharing the item. Time permitting, groups may share more than one attribute.

SINCE LAST WE MET

Since Last We Met is a metaphorical process used to capture the emotional tone of individual group members. On a chart or overhead transparency, write the phrase, "Since last we met, life has been like what book, movie or song title?" Each group member selects a book, movie or song title and develops an explanation for ways in which that choice captures his or her experiences.

www.miravia.com MiraVia, LLC • 3 Lost Acre Trail • Sherman CT 06784 860.354.4543

Paired Verbal Fluency*

Paired-Verbal Fluency is a strategy for getting participants verbally active at the start of a session. It can be used as a quick review of a prior session or as a jumpstart into that day's content. Establish pairs and have each team designate one partner as person 'A' and the other as person 'B'. Name the topic that each partner will discuss in turn. At your signal, person 'A' begins and talks until you say switch, at which point person 'B' takes over with the caveat that 'B' may not repeat anything that 'A' has all ready said. After an appropriate period of time elapses, say, "switch," for 'A' to again take over. Repeat this A–B pattern for three rounds using a decreasing amount of time for each round. Periods of 60–45–and 30 seconds for each partner will often be useful for energizing and focusing group members.

Value Voting*

Value Voting is a quick assessment of some aspect of group process or individual or group life. Participants raise their hands and indicate with one to five fingers how they feel about or rate a selected topic. Topics might include: rate your day or week thus far; rate your feelings about how productive our last session was; rate your sense of how we are progressing as a group; or rate your sense of optimism about what we will be able to accomplish today.

Banned Words

Banned Words are an energizing and often humorous way to start a session. Place a chart stand at the front of the room and ask group members to offer words or phrases that they would like to not hear during that day's activities. These will become "banned words" for that day. If a banned word is heard, the group is expected to groan loudly. Examples might include phrases like: "thinking outside the box," "research-based" or "exemplary practices."

Hopes and Fears

Hopes and Fears can be done individually, in pairs or in small groups. On chart paper or an overhead transparency draw a T-chart and head one column Hopes and the other column Fears. Ask participants to generate responses under each heading related to that session's topic or to the greater efforts of the group.

A–Z Listing

A–Z Listing is a quick idea generator that jumpstarts thinking and idea development. On chart paper or overhead transparency write the alphabet A–Z vertically down the left hand margin. Have small groups select recorders and use this template to generate words or short phrases beginning with each letter that relate to the topic before the group.

* These time-efficient strategies are also effective for ending a session.

APPENDIX E: *Types of Survey or Interview Questions*

Background/ Demographic Questions

Concern the interviewee's identifying characteristics

Are distinquished by their specific and somewhat routine nature

Examples: "How many years have you been teaching here?"

"What level of education have you completed?"

Experience/Behavior Questions

Ask about what a person does or has done

Elicit descriptions of observable experiences, behaviors, activities, actions

Example: "If I had been in the classroom with you, what might I have seen or heard?"

Knowledge Questions

Inquire about the respondent's perspective on empirical data

Seek factual information such as rules, regulations, program data, logistics, etc.

Examples: "How many planning periods are scheduled each week?"

"How many students are scheduled for special services?"

Cognitive Questions

Aim at understanding the cognitive and interpretive processes of people

Tell us about people's interpretations, analyses, inferences

Example: "What do you think about . . ."

Affective Questions

Seek to understand people's emotional responses to their experiences

Will often be responded to with adjectives (happy, responsible, intimidated, frustrated, etc.)

Examples: "How do you feel about . . ."

"What are your reactions to . . ."

Sensory Questions

Ask about what is seen, heard, touched, tasted and smelled

Elicit vivid descriptions or events or environments

Example: "When you walk into the classroom, what do you see?"

Identity/Value Questions

Seek expressions of identity, values and beliefs

Tell us about interviewee's goals, intentions, desires, values

Examples: "What do you value most about . . ."

"What would you most like to see happen?"

Role Play and Simulations

Provide a context for potentially difficult questions

Put the interviewee in the stance of expert

Reduce the personal nature of some questions

Examples: "Suppose I just started teaching here. What would be the most important things I would need to know to be successful?"

"Suppose you needed to get something done around here. What would you do?"

www.miravia.com MiraVia, LLC • 3 Lost Acre Trail • Sherman CT 06784 860.354.4543

APPENDIX F: Equipment Materials List

Presenter(s): _____

Session Title: _____ Date(s): _____

WORKSHOP NEEDS
This material and equipment list is for all scheduled sessions
Unless otherwise indicated, at each session, we will need:

Audio/Visual
__ wireless lapel microphone(s)
__ overhead projector and screen plus extension cord as needed
__ flip chart pads and chart stands
__ CD player—ideally connected to PA system
__ VHS VCR or DVD player and monitor(s)
__ LCD projector

Materials & Equipment
__ name tags
__ 3 x 5 index cards (about 10 per participant)
__ chisel point, water-based markers (a multi-colored six pack for every 4–6 participants)
__ blank transparencies and water-based transparency markers
__ masking tape
__ gluesticks
__ scissors, large
__ high-backed chair(s)

Note: At a hotel or conference center, you can usually get bar stools with backs from the hotel set-up crew.

Room Design
Tables arranged for groups of 4–6 (no larger, if at all possible)
Please set up in chevron (or reversed herringbone) as in Appendix G: Thinking About Room Design.

Note: Please be sure to give this diagram to the set up crew. It is important to set up the chairs and the table angle so no one's back is to the front.

Notes/Special Requests

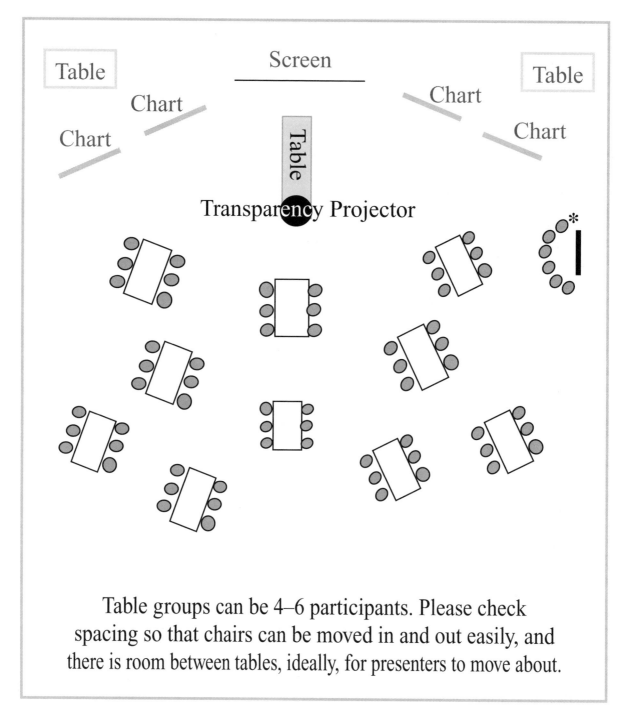

Table groups can be 4–6 participants. Please check spacing so that chairs can be moved in and out easily, and there is room between tables, ideally, for presenters to move about.

* Please be sure there is space around the perimeter of the room for "data stations". That is, a chart stand, or wall space for posting a chart, around which 6 chairs can be clustered. We will need one data station for every six participants (see sample above).

Note: Provide 25–30 square feet per participant when you select a meeting room.

References and Resources

REFERENCES

Argyris, C. (1990). *Overcoming organizational defenses: Facilitating organizational change,* Boston: Allyn and Bacon.

Arrow, H. & McGrath, J.E. (1993). Membership matters: How member change and continuity affect small group structure, process, and performance. *Small Group Research,* 24, 334–361.

Bandler, R. & Grinder, J. (1971). *The structure of magic.* Palo Alto, CA: Science and Behavior Books.

Beach, L. (1997). *The psychology of decision making: People in organizations.* Thousand Oaks, CA: Sage Publications.

Bernhardt, V. (1998). *Data analysis for comprehensive schoolwide improvement.* Larchmont, NY: Eye on Education Inc.

Bernhardt, V. (2000). *Designing and using databases for school improvement.* Larchmont, NY: Eye on Education Inc.

Black, P. & Wiliam, D. (1998). Inside the black box: Raising standards through classroom assessment. *Phi Delta Kappan,* October, 1998, 79(2), 139–148.

Bohm, D. (1990). *On dialogue.* Ojai, CA: David Bohm Seminars.

Bracey, G.W. (1997). *Understanding education statistics: Its easier (and more important) than you think.* Arlington, VA: Educational Research Service.

Bransford, J., Brown, A., & Cocking, R. (1999). *How people learn: Brain, mind, experience, and school.* Washington, DC: National Academy Press.

Bridges, W. (1991). *Managing transitions: Making the most of changes.* Boston, MA: Addison-Wesley.

Brody, H. (2000). T*he other side of eden: Hunters, farmers and the shaping of the world.* New York: North Point Press.

Calhoun, E. (1994). *How to use action research in the self-renewing school.* Alexandria, VA: Association for Supervision and Curriculum Development.

Capra, F. (1996). *The web of life: A new scientific understanding of living systems.* New York: Anchor Books, Doubleday.

Chang, F.Y. (1994). Schoolteachers' moral reasoning. In R. Houston (Ed). *Handbook of research on teacher education* (pp. 291–310). New York: Macmillan.

Cochran-Smith, M. & Lytle, S. (1990). Research on teaching and teacher research: The issues that divide. *Educational Researcher,* 19(2): 2–11.

Darling-Hammond, L. (1997). *The right to learn.* San Francisco: Jossey-Bass.

Doyle, M. & Straus, D. (1976). *How to make meetings work!* New York: Berkley Books.

Egawa, K. & Harste, J.C. (October 2001). Balancing the literary curriculum: A new vision. *SchoolTalk,* (7)1, 1–8.

Elgin, S.H. (2000). *The gentle art of verbal self-defense.* New York: Prentice-Hall.

Elmore, R.F. (2002a). *Bridging the gap between standards and achievement.* Washington, DC: The Albert Shanker Institute.

Elmore, R.F. (2002b). The limits of "change", *Harvard Education Letter* Jan./Feb. 2002, 18(1), 7–8.

Evans, R. (1996). *The human side of school change.* San Francisco: Jossey-Bass.

Frey. L. R. (1999). *The handbook of group communication theory & research.* Thousand Oaks. CA: Sage Publications, ix.

Fullan, M. (2001). *Leading in a culture of change.* San Francisco: Jossey-Bass.

Furman, S. (1999). The new accountability. *CPRE Policy Briefs.* RB–27-Jan. 1999, Philadelphia: University of Pennsylvania.

Garmston, R.J. & Wellman, B. (1999). *The adaptive school: A sourcebook for developing collaborative groups.* Norwood, MA: Christopher-Gordon.

Girgerenzer, G. & Seleten, R. (2001). *Bounded rationality: The adaptive toolbox.* Cambridge, MA: The MIT Press.

Goleman, D. (1994). *Emotional Intelligence: Why it can matter more than IQ.* New York: Bantam Books.

Grinder, M. (1997). *The science of nonverbal communication.* Battleground, WA: Michael Grinder and Associates.

Gronlund, N.E. & Linn, R.L. (1990). *Measurement and evaluation of teaching.* 6th ed. New York: Macmillan.

Guskey, T.R. & Bailey, J.M. (2001). *Developing grading and reporting systems for student learning.* Thousand Oaks, CA: Corwin.

Herman, J. & Winters, L. (1992). *Tracking your school's success: A guide to sensible evaluation.* Newbury Park, CA: Corwin Press.

Huberman, H. & Miles, M. (1984). *Qualitative data analysis: A sourcebook of new methods.* Beverly Hills, CA: Sage Publications.

Hunt, D. (1987). *Beginning with ourselves.* Cambridge, MA: Brookline Books.

Hurston, Z.N. (1942). *Dust on the Road,* New York: HarperCollins.

Isaacs, W. (1999). *Dialogue and the art of thinking together.* New York: Currency.

Jantsch, E. (1980). *The self-organizing universe.* Oxford: Pergamon.

Joyce, B., Wolf, J. & Calhoun, E. (1993). *The self-renewing school.* Alexandria, VA: Association for Supervision and Curriculum Development.

Kelsey, D. & Plumb. P. (2001). *Great meetings: How to facilitate like a pro.* Portland, ME: Hanson Park Press.

Kingsolver, B. (1998). *The poisonwood bible.* New York: HarperCollins.

Laborde, G.Z. (1984). *Influencing with integrity: Management skills for communication and negotiation.* Palo Alto, CA: Syntony.

Lipton, L., & Wellman, B. (2000). *Pathways to understanding: Patterns and practices in the learning-focused classroom.* Sherman, CT: MiraVia LLC.

Lipton, L., & Wellman, B. (2001). From staff development to professional development: Supporting thoughtful adults for thinking schools. A.L. Costa (Ed). *Developing minds: A resource book for teaching thinking.* (pp. 118–122). Arlington, VA: Association for Supervision and Curriculum Development.

Lipton, L., Wellman, B. & Humbard, C. (2003). *Mentoring matters: A practical guide to learning-focused relationships.* Sherman, CT: MiraVia.

Little, J.W. (1990). Teachers as colleagues. In A. Lieberman (Ed). *Schools as collaborative cultures: Creating the future now.* (pp. 165–193). New York: Palmer Press.

Lortie, D. (1975). *Schoolteacher: A sociological study.* Chicago: University of Chicago Press.

Louis, K.S., Kruse, S.D. & Marks, H.M. (1996). Teachers' professional community in restructuring schools. *American Educational Research Journal,* 33(1), 757–798.

Love, N. (2002). *Using data/getting results: A practical guide for school improvement in mathematics and science.* Norwood, MA: Christopher-Gordon.

Marzano, R.J. (2000). *Transforming classroom grading.* Alexandria, VA: Association for Supervision and Curriculum Development.

McAllister, G. & Irvine, J.J. (2000). Cross cultural competency and multicultural teacher education. *Review of Educational Research,* 70(1), 3–24.

McLaughlin, M.W., & Talbert, J.E. (2001). *Professional community and the work of high school teaching.* Chicago: University of Chicago Press.

Nave, B., Miech, E. & Mosteller, F. (2000). *A lapse in standards: Linking standards-based reform with student achievement.* Phi Delta Kappan, 82(2) October 2000, 128–132.

Newman, F., King, B. & Rigdon, M. (1997). Accountability and school performance: Implications from restructuring schools. *Harvard Educational Review,* 67(l), Spring, 41–74.

O'Connor, K. (2002). *How to grade for learning: Linking grades to standards.* Arlington Heights, IL: Skylight Professional Development.

Pacanowsky, M. (1995). Team tools for wicked problems. *Organizational Dynamics,* 23(3), Winter, 36–51.

Pajares, M.F. (1992). Teachers' beliefs and educational research: Cleaning up a messy construct. *Review of Educational Research,* 62(3), 307–332.

Payne, S. (1980). *The art of asking questions.* Princeton, NJ: Princeton University Press.

Patton, M. (1987). *Qualitative evaluation methods.* Beverly Hills, CA: Sage Publications.

Ross, R. & Roberts, C. (1994). Balancing advocacy and inquiry. In Senge, P., Ross, R., Smith, B. & Kleiner, A. *The fifth discipline fieldbook: Strategies and tools for building a learning organization.* (253–262). New York: Doubleday.

Rowe, M.B. (1986 January–February). Wait time: Slowing down may be a way of speeding up! *Journal of Teacher Education:* 43–49.

Sagor, R. (1992). *How to conduct collaborative action research.* Alexandria, VA: ASCD.

Sanders, W. L. & Rivers, J.C. (1996). *Cumulative and residual effects of teachers on future student academic achievement.* Knoxville, TN: University of Tennessee Value-Added Research and Assessment Center. Retrieved on January 5, 2003 from http://www.mdk12.org/practices/ensure/tva/tva_2.html.

Saphier, J. & Gower, R. (1997). *The skillful teacher: Building your teaching skills.* Carlisle, MA: Research for Better Teaching.

Sarason, S.B. (1990). *The predictable failure of educational reform,* San Francisco: Jossey-Bass.

Schlechty, P.C. (2001). *Shaking up the schoolhouse: How to support and sustain educational innovation.* San Francisco: Jossey-Bass.

Schoenfeld, A. H. (2002). Making mathematics work for all children: Issues of standards, testing, and equity. *Educational Researcher,* 31(1), 13–25.

Schwartz, R. M. (1994). *The skilled facilitator: Practical wisdom for developing effective groups.* San Francisco: Jossey-Bass Publishers, (4–6).

Selten, R. (2001). What is bounded rationality. In Girgerenzer, G. & Seleten, R. Ed,. Bounded rationality: *The adaptive toolbox,* Cambridge, MA: MIT Press.

Senge, P.M. (1990). *The fifth discipline: The art and practice of the learning organization.* New York: Doubleday-Currency.

Shulman, L.S. (1987). Knowledge and teaching: Foundations of the new reform. *Harvard Educational Review,* 57(1), 1–22.

Sparks, D. (2003). Honor the human heart (An interview with Parker J. Palmer), *JSD,* Summer 2003, 24(3), 49–53.

Stiggins, R.J. (1995). Assessment literacy for the 21st century. *Phi Delta Kappan,* November, 1995, 76(3), 238–245.

Todd, P. (2001). Fast and frugal heuristics for environmentally bounded minds. In Girgerenzer, G. & Selten, R. Ed,. *Bounded rationality: The adaptive toolbox,* Cambridge, MA: MIT Press.

Tomlinson, C. (2001). *How to differentiate instruction in mixed ability classrooms Second Edition.* Alexandria, VA: Association for Supervision and Curriculum Development.

Tufte, E. (1983). *The visual display of quantitative information.* Cheshire, CT: Graphics Press.

Tyack, D, & Cuban, L. (1995). *Tinkering towards utopia: A century of public school reform.* Cambridge, MA: Harvard University Press.

Wahlstrom, D. (1999). *Using data to improve student achievement.* Virginia Beach, VA: Successline.

Wenglinsky, H. (2002). *How teaching matters: Bringing the classroom back into discussions of teacher quality.* Princeton, NJ: Educational Testing Service.

Wheatley, M. J. (1999). *Leadership and the new science: Discovering order in a chaotic world.* San Francisco: Berrett-Koehler, (20).

Wiggins, G., & McTighe, J. (1998). *Understanding by design.* Alexandria, VA: Association for Supervision and Curriculum Development.

RESOURCES

COMMUNICATION/DIALOGUE

Burgoon, J.K., Buller, D.B. & Woodall. W.G. (1996). *Nonverbal communication: The unspoken dialogue.* New York: McGraw-Hill.

Burley-Allen, M. (1995). *Listening: The forgotten skill.* New York: John Wiley & Sons.

Donnellon, A. (1996). *Team talk: The power of language in team dynamics.* Cambridge, MA: Harvard Business School Press.

Ellinor, L. & Gerard, G. (1998). *Dialogue: Rediscovering the transforming power of conversation.* New York: John Wiley & Sons.

Grinder, M. (1995). *ENVoY: A personal guide to classroom management.* Battleground, WA: Michael Grinder and Associates.

Nichols, M.P. (1995). *The lost art of listening: How learning to listen can improve relationships.* New York: The Guilford Press.

Rosenberg, M.B. (1999). *Nonviolent communication: A language of compassion.* Encinitas, CA: PuddleDancer Press.

Stanfield, R.B. (2000). *The art of focused conversation: 101 ways to access group wisdom.* Gabriola Island, BC: New Society Publishers.

DATA TOOLS SOFTWARE

THE QUALITY SCHOOL PORTFOLIO. Developed by the National Center for Research on Evaluation Standards, and Student Testing (CRESST). Includes a data manager, which imports data from various sources and a tool kit, which offers surveys, interview protocols, and targeted questionnaires regarding critical school issues.

CRESST/UCLA 301 GSE&IS Box 951522, Los Angeles, CA 90095
http://qsp.cse.ucla.edu/

EDEXPLORE. Developed by Edsmart, Edexplore provides access to, and inquiry and analysis of a rich bank of district/ school related data. Educational staff can query the data in novel, nonlinear ways.

Edsmart 126 Cold Spring Road Avon, CT 06001 *www.edsmartinc.com*

SUCCESS FINDER. Developed by Evaluation Software Publishing, Success Finder is us a web-based performance management system for monitoring and reporting district/ school progress. In conjunction with Texas Business and Education Coalition

Evaluation Software Publishing 1510 W. 34th St Suite 209 Austin, TX 78703 *www.evalsoft.com*

FACILITATION

Benis, I. (2000). *Facilitating with ease!* San Francisco: Jossey-Bass.

Kaner, S. (1996). *Facilitator's guide to participatory decision-making.* Gabriola Island, BC: New Society Publishers.

Kelsey, D. & Plumb, P. (2001). *Great meetings: How to facilitate like a pro.* Portland, ME: Hanson Park Press.

Silberman, M. (1999). *101 ways to make meetings active.* San Francisco: Jossey-Bass/Pfeiffer.

Schwartz, R.M. (1994). *The skilled facilitator: Practical wisdom for developing effective groups.* San Francisco: Jossey-Bass.

Tropman, J.E. (1996). *Making meetings work: Achieving high quality group decisions.* Thousand Oaks, CA: Sage Publications.

GROUP DEVELOPMENT/GROUP PROCESSES

Achinstein, B. (2002). *Community, diversity and conflict among schoolteachers: The ties that bind.* New York: Teachers College Press.

Argyris, C. (1990). *Overcoming organizational defenses: Facilitating organizational learning.* Needham Heights, MA: Allyn and Bacon.

Arrow, H., McGrath, J.E. & Berdahl, H. L. (2000). *Small groups as complex systems: Formation, coordination, development, and adaptation.* Thousand Oaks, CA: Sage Publications.

Bryk, A.S. & Schneider, B. (2002). *Trust in schools: A core resource for improvement.* New York: Russell Sage Foundation.

Hirokawa, R.Y. & Poole, M.S. (1996). *Communication and group decision making.* Thousand Oaks, CA: Sage Publications.

Holcomb, E. (1996). *Asking the right questions: Tools and techniques for teamwork.* Thousand Oaks, CA: Corwin Press.

Hunter, D., Bailey, A. & Taylor, B. (1995). *The Zen of groups: The handbook for people meeting with a purpose.* Tucson, AZ: Fisher Books.

Robbins, H. & Finley, M. (2000). *The new why teams don't work: What goes wrong and how to make it right.* San Francisco: Berrett-Koehler.

Zander, A. (1994). *Making groups effective.* San Francisco: Jossey-Bass.

WORKING WITH DATA

Banyai, I. (1995). *Zoom.* New York: Viking Press.

Bracey, G.W. (2000). *Bail me out!: Handling difficult data and tough questions about public schools.* Thousand Oaks, CA: Corwin Press.

Holcomb, E. (1998). *Getting excited about data.* Thousand Oaks, CA: Corwin Press.

Leithwood, K. & Aitken, R. (1995). *Making schools smarter: A system for monitoring school and district progress.* Thousand Oaks, CA: Corwin Press.

McClanahan, E., & Wicks, C. (1993). *Future force: Kids that want to, can and do!: A teacher's handbook for using TQM in the classroom.* Chino Hills, CA: PACT Publishing.

ON-LINE RESOURCES

Center for Accountability Solutions: *www.aasa.org/issues-and-insights/technology/cas.htm*

Assists school leaders in gathering, analysing and reporting on data related to student, school and district performance.

National Center for Research on Evaluation Standards, and Student Testing (CRESST): *www.cse.ucla.edu/*

Conducts and describes research on a variety of educational topics related to K–12 testing.

New Horizons for Learning: *http://www.newhorizons.org*
Presents articles and information on a range of current issues in education. Site includes an online journal and downloadable files from a variety of text sources.

FINDING TIME

Many groups struggle with finding ways to make or protect time for collaborative work. These websites off tips and rationale for both the need for collaborative time and practical examples of ways schools have made this happen.

National Staff Development Council: *www.nsdc.org/library/time.html*
Association for Supervision and Curriculum Development: *www.ascd.org/readingroom/edlead/9309/raywid.html*

INDEX

ABOUT THE AUTHORS

Bruce Wellman, M.Ed, Co-Director of *MiraVia, LLC*

Bruce Wellman consults with school systems, professional groups and
publishers throughout the United States and Canada, presenting
workshops and courses for teachers and administrators on teaching
methods and materials, thinking skills development, Learning-Focused
Mentoring, presentation skills and facilitating collaborative groups. Mr.
Wellman has served as a classroom teacher, curriculum coordinator and
staff developer in the Oberlin, Ohio, and Concord, Massachusetts public
schools. He holds a B.A. degree from Antioch College and an M.Ed
from Lesley College.

Contact Bruce at:
229 Colyer Road • Guilford, VT • 05301
P: **802.257.4892** • *F:* **802.257.2403** • *e-mail:* **bwellman@miravia.com**

Laura Lipton, Ed.D, Co-Director of *MiraVia, LLC*

Laura Lipton is an instructional strategist who specializes in curriculum
and instructional design to promote thinking, learning and thoughtful
assessment. Her broad teaching background includes K-12 general and
special education and teacher preparation courses. Dr. Lipton has
extensive experience in literacy development, curriculum, thinking skills
development, thoughtful assessment and Learning-Focused Mentoring.
She leads workshops and seminars throughout the United States,
Canada, Europe, Australia and New Zealand.

Contact Laura at:
3 Lost Acre Trail • Sherman, CT • 06784
P: **860.354.4543** • *F:* **860.354.6740** • *e-mail:* **lelipton@miravia.com**

Professional Development Programs and Services
Putting Theory into Practice in Your Schools

MiraVia provides learning-focused professional development programs and services that present practical strategies, useful resources and innovative ideas for thoughtful educators grappling with critical professional issues.

Seminars • Keynotes • Consulting Services

Developing Learning-Focused Relationships

Target Audience: Teacher mentors, instructional and content coaches, curriculum specialists and instructional supervisors

Explore the essential concepts, templates and mediational tools for developing effective, learning-focused relationships between growth-oriented educators.

Workshops and seminars include:

- Mentoring Matters: A Practical Guide to Learning-Focused Relationships
- Learning-Focused Relationships: Coaching, Collaborating and Consulting for Professional Excellence
- Learning-focused Supervision: Calibrating Professional Excellence

Building Professional Community

Target Audience: School and district leaders, site and district teams, facilitators and group developers

Learn critical skills for developing collaborative school cultures that focus on the learning needs of students and the adults who serve them.

Workshops and seminars include:

- Data-Driven Dialogue: Facilitating Collaborative Inquiry
- Leading Groups: Framing, Presenting, Collaborating and Facilitating
- Learning-Focused Presentations
- The Facilitator's Toolkit: Balancing Task, Process and Relationship
- Teacher to Teacher: Working Collaboratively for Student Success

Creating Learning-Focused Classrooms and Schools

Target Audience: Beginning and experienced classroom teachers, staff developers, instructional leaders

Discover the bridge between current learning theory and effective classroom practice. Our research-based and classroom-tested Pathways Learning Model offers a coherent framework for organizing lessons and units of study.

Workshops and seminars include:

- Pathways to Understanding: Patterns and Practices in the Learning-Focused Classroom
- Pathways to Literacy: Reading and Writing in the Content Areas
- Getting Started, Getting Smarter: Practical Tools for Beginning Teachers
- Thinking to Learn, Learning to Think

Specialty Seminars

Institute for Leaders and Learners

Extend and enhance your skills at this 5-day institute, *Learning-Focused Relationships: Consulting, Collaborating and Coaching for Professional Excellence*. Be part of this high-energy, high-engagement forum as you learn to apply patterns and practices for creating and sustaining learning-focused relationships between professional colleagues, use data to focus attention and energy, and increase skill in planning and problem-solving.

Orientation Session—Learning-Focused Mentoring: A Professional Development Resource Kit

Maximize the effectiveness of *Learning-Focused Mentoring: A Professional Development Resource Kit* by participating in an orientation session led by experienced users. These sessions illuminate the print and media resources contained in this comprehensive kit, provide tips and techniques for artful application, deepen mentoring skill and content understanding and offer practical strategies for presenting to adult learners.

Enhancing Your Visual Appeal 1
Creating Powerful Presentation Graphics

Enhancing Your Visual Appeal 2
From Plain to Powerful: Adding Impact to your Printed Materials

Presented by Michael Buckley – Designer of ChartArt©

These practical and engaging sessions offer hands-on experience in creating effective presentation visuals and attention grabbing graphics for your professional documents. Expertly guided by an experienced and award-winning graphic designer and illustrator, these lively sessions offer tools and templates for increasing the impact of your workshop charts, handouts, transparencies and printed materials.

MiraVia offers seminars in a variety of formats for customized programs that meet client needs and outcomes:

Awareness Sessions: 1-2 days
Foundation Seminars: 4-6 days
Advanced Seminars: 2-4 days

We tailor consulting services for school improvement planning and project design to meet specific client requirements.

For information

On Professional Development

Laura Lipton   or   Bruce Wellman
lelipton@miravia.com   bwellman@miravia.com
860-354-4543   802-257-4892

About Our Products

e-mail   info@miravia.com
phone   781-316-8484
fax   781-998-0298

or visit our website www.miravia.com

About MiraVia®   The Road to Learning

mira (L.)[MIR-â]: wonderful/amazing   via (L.)[VE-â]: way or road

IN 1596, the German astronomer Fabricus saw a third magnitude star in the constellation Cetus, the Whale. As they continued to observe it over the next century, astronomers became aware of its unusual fluctuations, now brighter, now fading, and honored it with the name Mira, the Wonderful.

As a partnership dedicated to continued development for professionals, we connect the constancy of presence and fluctuating brightness with the learning process. We believe that learning means working through the temporary dullness of not knowing, while pursuing the brilliance of new understanding. Our name, and our philosophy, combines this wonder of learning, Mira, with Via, or the road. Our publications, products and seminars offer pathways to professional insight and growth.